# Adobe® InDesign® CC: Part 2

# Adobe® InDesign® CC: Part 2

Part Number: 092024
Course Edition: 9.0

## Acknowledgements

### PROJECT TEAM

| Author | Media Designer | Content Editor |
|---|---|---|
| Gail Sandler | Brian Sullivan | Michelle Farney |

## Notices

### DISCLAIMER

### TRADEMARK NOTICES

# Adobe® InDesign® CC: Part 2

# About This Course

In *Adobe® InDesign® CC: Part 1* you were introduced to the many features that help you create professional looking documents. Now you need to create much lengthier interactive documents that need to be accessed across a range of devices. In *Adobe® InDesign® CC: Part 2*, you will learn advanced InDesign techniques to enhance the look and functionality of your documents.

Using Adobe InDesign, you can create interactive documents and export them for viewing in a web browser with various features such as buttons, page transitions, movies and audio files, hyperlinks, and animation. You have the ability to assign color profiles and establish print presets. In creating longer documents, you'll be able to include such features as a table of contents, footnotes, cross-references, and an index.

This course is a great component of your preparation for the Adobe Certified Professional Print & Digital Media Publication Using Adobe InDesign CC exam.

## Course Description

### Target Student

This course is intended for students who want to expand their entry-level knowledge of Adobe InDesign by using advanced features and collaboration tools. It's also for anyone interested in working toward the Print & Digital Media Publication Using Adobe InDesign certification.

### Course Prerequisites

To ensure your success, you will need to take the following Logical Operations course:

*   *Adobe® InDesign® CC: Part 1*

### Course Objectives

Upon successful completion of this course, you will be able to use Adobe InDesign CC to create and deliver professional looking printed and interactive documents.

You will:

*   Prepare documents for multiple formats.
*   Manage advanced page layouts.
*   Manage styles.
*   Build complex paths.
*   Manage external files and create dynamic documents.
*   Manage long documents.
*   Publish InDesign files for other formats and customize print settings.

# The CHOICE Home Screen

Logon and access information for your CHOICE environment will be provided with your class experience. The CHOICE platform is your entry point to the CHOICE learning experience, of which this course manual is only one part.

On the CHOICE Home screen, you can access the CHOICE Course screens for your specific courses. Visit the CHOICE Course screen both during and after class to make use of the world of support and instructional resources that make up the CHOICE experience.

Each CHOICE Course screen will give you access to the following resources:

- **Classroom**: A link to your training provider's classroom environment.
- **eBook**: An interactive electronic version of the printed book for your course.
- **Files**: Any course files available to download.
- **Checklists**: Step-by-step procedures and general guidelines you can use as a reference during and after class.
- **LearnTOs**: Brief animated videos that enhance and extend the classroom learning experience.
- **Assessment**: A course assessment for your self-assessment of the course content.
- Social media resources that enable you to collaborate with others in the learning community using professional communications sites such as LinkedIn or microblogging tools such as Twitter.

Depending on the nature of your course and the components chosen by your learning provider, the CHOICE Course screen may also include access to elements such as:

- LogicalLABS, a virtual technical environment for your course.
- Various partner resources related to the courseware.
- Related certifications or credentials.
- A link to your training provider's website.
- Notices from the CHOICE administrator.
- Newsletters and other communications from your learning provider.
- Mentoring services.

Visit your CHOICE Home screen often to connect, communicate, and extend your learning experience!

# How to Use This Book

## As You Learn

This book is divided into lessons and topics, covering a subject or a set of related subjects. In most cases, lessons are arranged in order of increasing proficiency.

The results-oriented topics include relevant and supporting information you need to master the content. Each topic has various types of activities designed to enable you to solidify your understanding of the informational material presented in the course. Information is provided for reference and reflection to facilitate understanding and practice.

Data files for various activities as well as other supporting files for the course are available by download from the CHOICE Course screen. In addition to sample data for the course exercises, the course files may contain media components to enhance your learning and additional reference materials for use both during and after the course.

Checklists of procedures and guidelines can be used during class and as after-class references when you're back on the job and need to refresh your understanding.

At the back of the book, you will find a glossary of the definitions of the terms and concepts used throughout the course. You will also find an index to assist in locating information within the instructional components of the book.

## As You Review

Any method of instruction is only as effective as the time and effort you, the student, are willing to invest in it. In addition, some of the information that you learn in class may not be important to you immediately, but it may become important later. For this reason, we encourage you to spend some time reviewing the content of the course after your time in the classroom.

## As a Reference

The organization and layout of this book make it an easy-to-use resource for future reference. Taking advantage of the glossary, index, and table of contents, you can use this book as a first source of definitions, background information, and summaries.

## Course Icons

Watch throughout the material for the following visual cues.

| Icon | Description |
|------|-------------|
|      | A **Note** provides additional information, guidance, or hints about a topic or task. |
|      | A **Caution** note makes you aware of places where you need to be particularly careful with your actions, settings, or decisions so that you can be sure to get the desired results of an activity or task. |
|      | **LearnTO** notes show you where an associated LearnTO is particularly relevant to the content. Access LearnTOs from your CHOICE Course screen. |
|      | **Checklists** provide job aids you can use after class as a reference to perform skills back on the job. Access checklists from your CHOICE Course screen. |
|      | **Social** notes remind you to check your CHOICE Course screen for opportunities to interact with the CHOICE community using social media. |

# 1 Preparing Documents for Multiple Formats

**Lesson Time: 30 minutes**

## Lesson Introduction

As technology advances, you'll find you have more and more ways in which you can deliver your documents. Gone are the days when print was the only option. Designers must take into account the various formats in which people will access the material. In this lesson, you will build layout versions and link content.

## Lesson Objectives

In this lesson, you will:

- Build layout versions.
- Link content.

# TOPIC A

## Build Layout Versions

Designers increasingly need to build for multiple device delivery. Adobe® InDesign® has the tools necessary to get this done. There are also some new tools added for Creative Cloud that make the reconfiguring of layouts that much easier. In this topic, you'll build layout versions.

### The Page Tool

The **Page** tool 🗔 can be used to select a parent page or layout page that you need to resize. You can use the **Control** panel to change the settings. Pages inherit their size from the parent page they're based on, but you can change the size of the layout page so that it's different from the parent.

### The Pages Panel

The **Pages** panel displays page thumbnails in various icon sizes for both *document pages* and parent pages. It allows you to navigate to pages, and when you move document pages to a new location, the **Pages** panel automatically scrolls to pages that are out of view. The **Pages** panel is used to create, delete, and apply parent pages to document pages. You may also insert, move, duplicate, rotate, and delete document pages using the **Pages** panel.

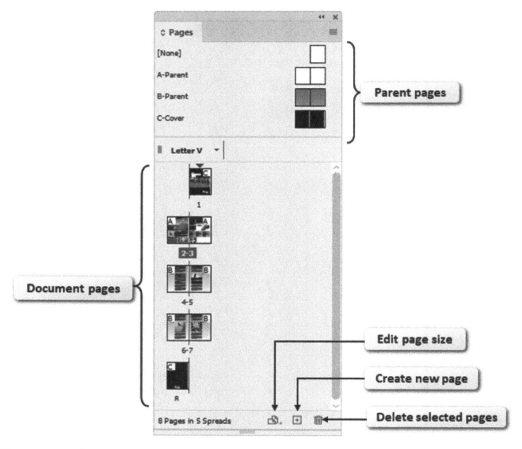

*Figure 1-1: The Pages panel.*

As you view the thumbnails in the **Pages** panel, you can also assign color labels to those thumbnails. These are useful if you wanted to use colors to indicate the status of a page. For example, a green thumbnail could be one that is completed. Yellow could be for one that is in progress. Red could be for one that has not been started, etc. To assign a label to a thumbnail, select the thumbnail in the **Pages** panel, and then from the panel menu, select **Page Attributes→Color Label**.

### Adding, Deleting, and Moving Pages

To add a document page, you can select **Insert Pages** from the **Pages** panel options menu. To create a new page based on a parent, click and drag that parent page into the document thumbnail area of the **Pages** panel. To delete a page, select it and select the **Delete selected pages** button. To move a page, you need only click and drag that page icon to the new position.

## Liquid Layouts

Liquid layouts allow you to design content for multiple page sizes, orientations, or devices. To do this, you apply rules to determine how objects on a page are adapted when you change the size, orientation, or aspect ratio. You're able to apply different rules to different pages. Liquid layout is a general term that covers a set of specific layout rules.

## Liquid Page Rules

Liquid page rules are the specific rules you apply to a page to determine how they adapt when resized. You can apply different rules to different pages. Only one liquid page rule can be applied to a page at a time.

There is a set of specific liquid page rules that you can adjust the settings for.

| Rule | Description |
| --- | --- |
| Scale | All content on the page is treated as a group, and as the page resizes, all elements scale in proportion. |
| Object-based | You specify liquid behavior for size and location relative to the page edge for each object, either fixed or relative. |
| Guide-based | Guides define a straight line across the page where content can adapt. |

### Pinning and Locking

When you apply object-based liquid layout rules, you do so by using pins represented by lines that radiate out from all sides of an object and end in a circle. Selecting that circle with the mouse pointer will lock or unlock the size or its position relative to one of the page edges.

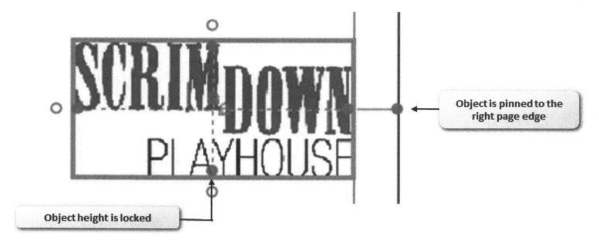

*Figure 1-2: Object-based liquid layout rules applied to size and location using pins.*

## The Liquid Layout Panel

The **Liquid Layout** panel is another place for you to define the settings for how objects will behave when the page is resized. Each of the four liquid page rules available in the **Liquid Page Rule** drop-down menu offers options specific to that rule.

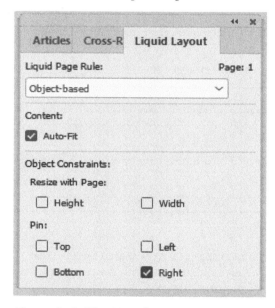

*Figure 1-3: The Liquid Layout panel showing the settings for an object-based liquid layout rule.*

## Alternate Layouts

**Alternate Layouts** is the feature you'll need if you require different page sizes for print or digital publishing within the same document. For instance, you could build different sizes of the same newspaper advertisement. Another would be to create horizontal and vertical layouts for use with tablets and smartphones.

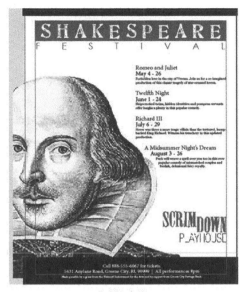
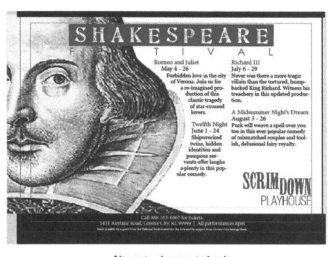

Original size

Alternate size created using
Liquid Layout rules

*Figure 1-4: Alternate layouts.*

## The Create Alternate Layout Dialog Box

The **Create Alternate Layout** dialog box is available from the **Pages** panel options menu, and can also be accessed by selecting **Layout→Create Alternate Layout**. The options it displays are determined by the **Intent** that was selected when you created the document.

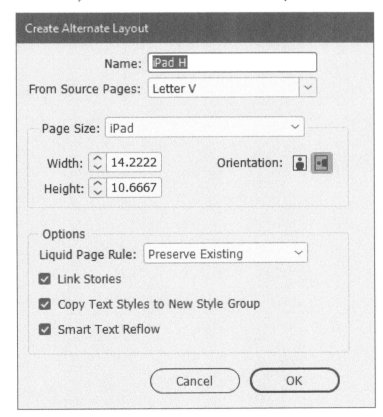

*Figure 1-5: The Create Alternate Layout dialog box based on a document with print intent selected.*

**Note:** To learn more about digital publishing with InDesign, check out the LearnTO **Optimize Your Designs for Digital Publishing** presentation from the **LearnTO** tile on the CHOICE Course screen.

 **Access the Checklist tile on your CHOICE Course screen for reference information and job aids on How to Build Layout Versions.**

# ACTIVITY 1–1
## Building Alternate Layouts of a Document

### Data File

C:\092024Data\Preparing Documents for Multiple Formats\Flyer.indd

### Scenario

You are the graphic designer in the marketing department of the Scrimdown Playhouse. You've already developed a one-page flyer, and now you'd like to adapt it for viewing on mobile devices like the iPad®.

 **Note:** Activities may vary slightly if the software vendor has issued digital updates. Your instructor will notify you of any changes.

---

1. Open **Flyer.indd**.

   a) Select **File→Open**. Navigate to the folder **C:\092024Data\Preparing Documents for Multiple Formats** and open the file **Flyer.indd**.

    **Note:** If prompted to update links, select **Update Links**.

   b) If necessary, from the **Workspace** drop-down list, select **Essentials Classic**.

   c) If rulers are not visible, select **View→Show Rulers** or press **Ctrl+R**.

2. Assign liquid page rules.

   a) In the **Tools** panel, select the **Page** tool.

   b) In the **Control** panel, from the **Liquid Page Rule** drop-down list, select **Object-based**.

   c) Select the black rectangle at the top of the page and pin its position relative to the top page edge by selecting the open circle.

    **Note:** Use the mouse to view tooltips that define each circle's purpose. Tooltips will also tell you whether the object is pinned/moveable, or whether the dimensions are locked/flexible.

   d) Hover over the closed circles and verify that the object's width is locked.

   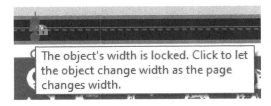

   The object's width is locked. Click to let the object change width as the page changes width.

---

e) Unlock the width of the top black rectangle by selecting the filled-in brown circle at far left so that it now appears open.

f) Select the black rectangle at the bottom of the page and pin it relative to the bottom page edge, as well as making its width flexible.

g) Select the image of Shakespeare. If necessary, unlock the height and width dimensions so they will resize using the mouse and pop-up tooltips.

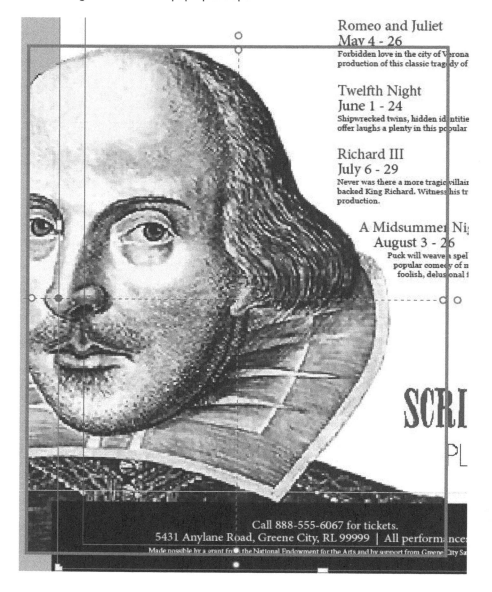

h) Select the logo image. Drag the right-side circle to the page edge to pin the right edge relative to the right page edge.

3. Add an alternate layout for iPad to the document.

   a) From the list of collapsed panels, open the **Pages** panel.

   Alternatively, you can select **Windows→Pages**.

   b) From the **Pages** panel options menu, select **Create Alternate Layout**.

   c) In the **Create Alternate Layout** dialog box, from the **Page Size** drop-down list, verify that **iPad** is selected.

   d) Verify that the orientation is set to **Landscape** and that in the **Liquid Page Rule** drop-down box, **Preserve Existing** is selected.

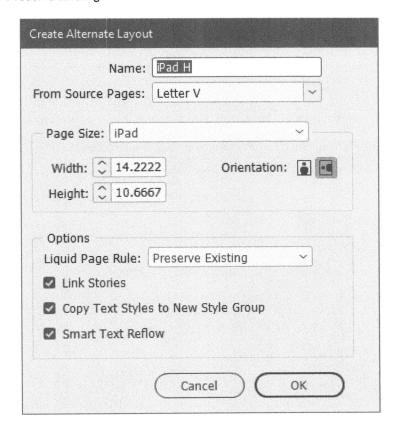

   e) Select **OK**.

4. Manually adjust the alternate iPad layout.

a) In the **Pages** panel, select the **iPad H** layout thumbnail image to open the alternate layout.

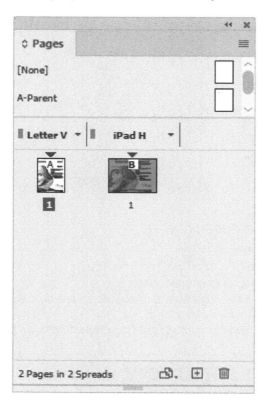

> **Note:** "iPad H" stands for "iPad Horizontal."

b) Observe that the various elements need to be resized and repositioned for the new layout.

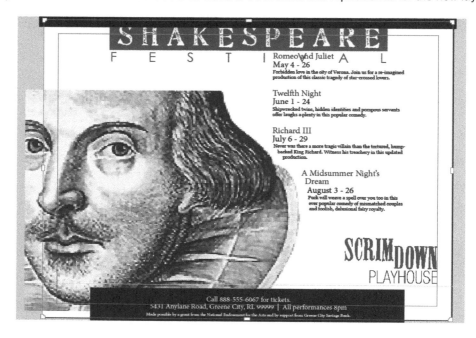

c) Using the **Selection** tool, resize and reposition the image of Shakespeare and the top and bottom black bars so that they fill the space and still bleed off the edge of the page.

**Note:** You might need to copy the top black bar from the Letter V layout and paste it into the iPad H layout.

d) Select the text box containing the performance information. Right-click the edge of the text frame and select **Text Frame Options**. In the **Columns** section, in the **Number** box, type *2* and then select **OK**.

e) Using the **Text** tool and the **Selection** tool, re-size the text and resize/reposition the text box as needed. With the **Text** tool selected, in the **Control** panel, change the font size and leading as needed to achieve the desired effect. Your results should be similar to the following image.

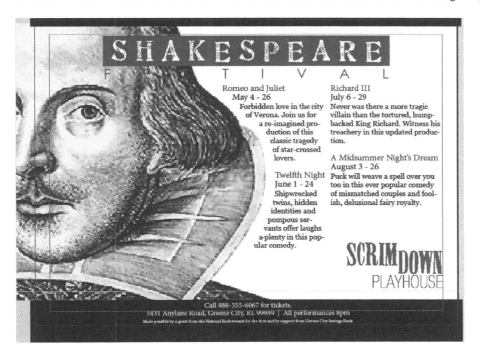

5. Save the file in the **C:\092024Data\Preparing Documents for Multiple Formats** folder as *My Flyer.indd*

6. Close the file.

# TOPIC B

## Link Content

A key to maintaining consistency and working efficiently is to reuse content where possible. InDesign allows you to re-purpose text and graphics and link them to the original so that you can be alerted of updates. In this topic, you will link content.

### The Content Collector and Content Placer Tools

The **Content Collector** and **Content Placer** tools allow you to duplicate objects and place them in open InDesign documents. As the objects are collected, they are displayed in the **Content Conveyor** where they can be easily identified and placed as needed.

*Figure 1-6: Content Collector and Content Placer tools.*

### Place and Link

There is also an option to **Link** these objects within a document or even across any open documents. To do this you may either choose **Edit→Place and Link** or in the **Tools** panel, select the **Content Collector** or **Content Placer** tools.

### The Content Conveyor

The **Content Conveyor** appears when you choose **Edit→Place and Link** or use the **Content Collector** or **Content Placer** tools. The conveyor displays thumbnails of the available objects. Buttons along the bottom provide options to link the content and map styles. There are also settings to have the content disappear after being placed or remain to be placed repeatedly.

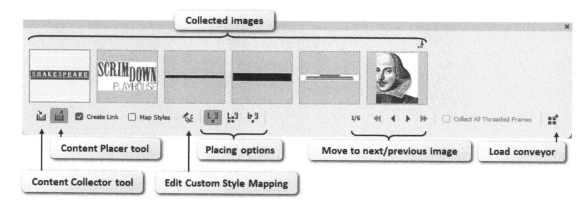

*Figure 1-7: The Content Conveyor with two objects displayed.*

# Link Options

**Link Options** are enabled when an object has been placed and linked. From the **Links** panel options menu, select **Link Options**. There you'll find settings for updates and warning messages. You can also select settings to preserve local edits.

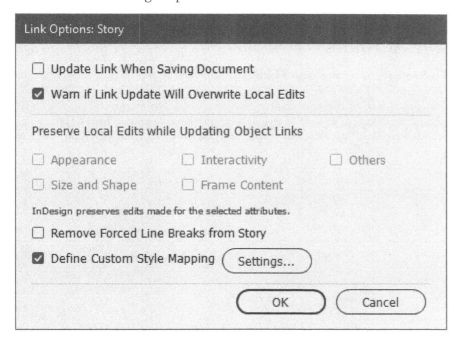

*Figure 1-8: The Link Options dialog box.*

### Link to Spreadsheet Files

When importing tables from another file, such as a spreadsheet, you can maintain a link to the original file. When the original file has been edited, a warning in the **Links** panel will notify you that the imported file needs to be updated. To do this, in the **File Handling** preference settings, select the **Create Links When Placing Text And Spreadsheet Files** option.

## Embedded Files

An alternative option to linking to external graphics is to embed them in your InDesign file. This way, the graphic is actually in the InDesign file. Embedding an image is done by selecting the image and then selecting **Embed Link** from the **Links** panel menu. It is important to note that if you embed your graphics, your InDesign file will grow in size and it also becomes difficult to edit the graphic. For this reason, embedding files is best left to smaller, less complex images.

## Update Link

InDesign notifies you in the **Links** panel when the link to an object is missing or out of date. These links can be identified by the **Modified link** icon. To update all modified links, from the **Links** panel menu, select **Update All Links**. Sometimes a graphic may appear in several places within the document. It's possible to just update one instance of the graphic by just selecting the sub-link and selecting **Update Link**. Selecting the parent link will update all links to the modified graphic.

# Relinked Graphics

You may want to change the source file that the graphic is linked to. To do this, select the **Relink** button 🔗 or choose **Relink** from the **Links** panel menu. In the dialog box, InDesign lets you browse to the new file to change the link.

# Metadata and File Attributes

At the bottom of the **Links** panel, you can expand **Link Info** to view a range of file attributes and metadata. This area is not editable but can be useful when you need information about a particular graphic or other linked object. Some of these attributes are the name, format, page(s) on which it appears, its status, the date it was placed, as well as the date it may have been modified. Different linked objects include various types of information stored with the object and displayed in the **Link Info** pane.

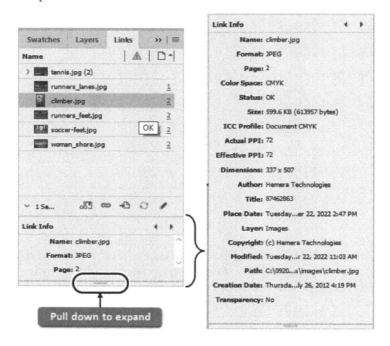

*Figure 1-9: The Link Info pane.*

> **Access the Checklist tile on your CHOICE Course screen for reference information and job aids on How to Link Content.**

# ACTIVITY 1-2
## Linking Content

### Data Files

C:\092024Data\Preparing Documents for Multiple Formats\Sports Brochure.indd

C:\092024Data\Preparing Documents for Multiple Formats\Business Card.indd

### Scenario

You have recently designed a new brochure for a sporting goods store and they're very happy with it. They would like you to redesign their business cards to follow the same style.

---

1. Navigate to the folder **C:\092024Data\Preparing Documents for Multiple Formats** and open the files **Sports Brochure.indd** and **Business Card.indd**.

    **Note:** If prompted to update links, select **Update Modified Links**. If prompted to find missing fonts, select **Activate**. When the font is successfully activated, select **Close**.

2. Collect and place content from the brochure into the business card.

   a) With the **Sports Brochure.indd** tab active, in the document window, navigate to page 1.

   b) In the **Tools** panel, select the **Content Collector** tool. The Content Conveyor appears at the bottom of the screen.

   c) With the **Content Collector** tool, select the text frame containing the text "Getting where you're going."

   Some of the text is white, so it will look like only "Getting" was placed in the **Content Conveyor**, but the rest of the text is there.

   d) Scroll down and also select the text frame with the logo "my footprint sports."

3. Place content in the Business card.indd document.

   a) Switch to the **Business Card.indd** tab, and in the document window, navigate to page 2.

   b) In the **Content Conveyor** window, select the **Content Placer** tool.

   c) Check the **Create Link** check box to enable it.

   d) With the mouse pointer loaded with the first conveyor element, on page 2, click in the pasteboard area to the left or right of the black rectangle.

e) You will get a message asking you to save the linked file. In the message box, select **OK**. Make sure the **Sports Brochure.indd** file is active and save the file as *My Sports Brochure.indd* inside the folder **C:\092024Data\Preparing Documents for Multiple Formats**.

f) Return to **Business Card.indd**, and if necessary, click again in the pasteboard area to the left or right of the black rectangle to paste the content.

g) With the **Selection** tool, reposition the text frame "Getting where you're going." on top of the black rectangle.

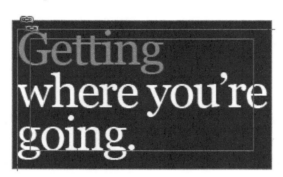

h) In the **Content Conveyor**, verify that the next image is ready for placement.

4. Navigate to page 1. With the mouse pointer loaded with the second gallery element, click in the area above the existing text.

5. Change the color of the white text to black.

a) Using the **Selection** tool, reposition the logo to the top and left margins.

b) Select the **Text** tool.

c) Highlight the text "my."

The text is currently white, so it isn't visible. You can see the outline of the text box above the word "footprint", so drag in the box above footprint to select the text.

d) In the **Tools** panel, double-click the **Fill** tool 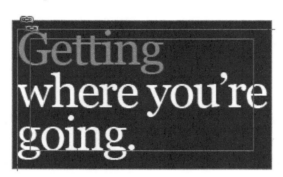 to open the **Color Picker**.

e) In the **Color Picker** dialog box, change all the **RGB** settings to *0* and observe that the color is now black.

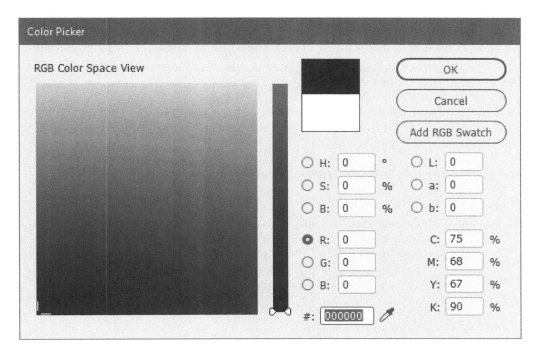

f) Select **OK**.
g) Repeat steps c through f for the text "sports."
h) Observe that the text "my" and "sports" has changed from white to black.

i) Save the file in the **C:\092024Data\Preparing Documents for Multiple Formats** folder as *My Business Card.indd*

6. Close both files.

# Summary

In this lesson, you learned of how InDesign's Liquid Layouts and Alternative Layouts can aid in the production of documents that are to be delivered to multiple devices. You also learned that linking content can enable you to repurpose images or text and still link them from the original so that you are alerted of updates to the content.

## How can you best take advantage of Alternate Layouts?

## When would having linked content be advantageous?

 **Note:** Check your CHOICE Course screen for opportunities to interact with your classmates, peers, and the larger CHOICE online community about the topics covered in this course or other topics you are interested in. From the Course screen you can also access available resources for a more continuous learning experience.

# 2 Managing Advanced Page Elements

**Lesson Time: 1 hour**

## Lesson Introduction

*Adobe® InDesign® CC: Part 1* introduced you to the software and got you started creating documents, but there's so much more to discover that can bring those documents to the next level. As a designer, you'll want to spend more time enhancing the formatting of the text in your document, as well as possibly include graphic motifs that repeat throughout the document. Additionally, the graphics in your documents can be adjusted to include transparency effects, such as drop shadows and embossing, and be anchored to flow with the text. Once you've created these graphics, you can build a library to use them in future documents. This lesson will discuss repeating elements, typography, building transparency, anchoring objects, and using a library.

## Lesson Objectives

In this lesson, you will:

- Create repeating content.

- Work with text layouts.

- Create transparency.

- Anchor objects and manage a library.

# TOPIC A

## Create Repeating Content

There will come a time as you design when you'll need to make a repeating element in your document that will appear on every page or just certain pages. In this topic, you will step through creating a repeating element in your document.

### Parent Page Creation

A *parent page* is a page that allows users to define the layout of document pages. It consists of text and images which will appear on multiple pages of a document. All new documents initially contain only one parent page, labeled A-Parent. Parent pages can be edited like any document page. Any change made to a parent page will reflect on every document page that is based on that parent. Additional parent pages can be added and applied to document pages. You can create parent pages based on other parent pages.

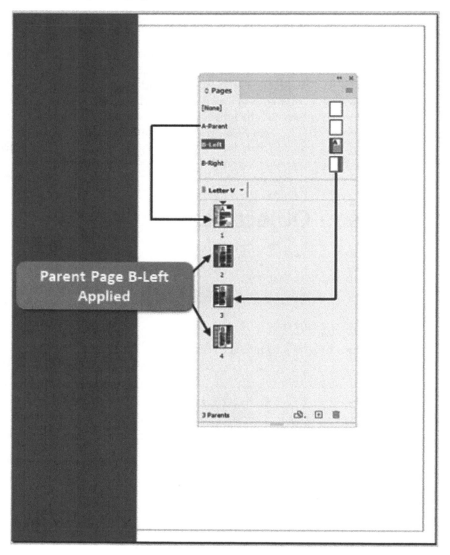

*Figure 2–1: Parent page creation.*

# Parent Page Editing

One of the primary benefits of the parent page is that you can apply changes to it and those changes will be made throughout the document. These changes can include adding a logo, headers, or page numbers to your document. This makes editing the parent page a quick and easy way to edit multiple pages in your InDesign document.

# Parent Page Override

Overriding a parent item puts a copy of it on the document page without breaking its association with the parent page. Once the item itself is overridden, you can selectively override one or more attributes of the item to customize it. For example, you can change the fill color of the local copy but when changes are made to the copy on the parent page, the fill color attribute will no longer update while other attributes like size or stroke will update. Overrides can be removed later to make the object match the parent.

 **Access the Checklist tile on your CHOICE Course screen for reference information and job aids on How to Create Repeating Content.**

# ACTIVITY 2–1
## Creating Repeating Content

### Data File

C:\092024Data\Managing Advanced Page Elements\Nursery Newsletter.indd

### Scenario

You've been asked to develop a monthly newsletter for your daughter's nursery school. Since this will be a regularly updated document, you'd like to take advantage of features in InDesign that allow you to create repeating elements on multiple pages.

1. Navigate to the folder **C:\092024Data\Managing Advanced Page Elements** and open the file **Nursery Newsletter.indd**.

>  **Note:** If prompted to update links, select **Update Modified Links.**

2. Create a new parent page.
   a) If necessary, on the **Application** bar, select **Window→Pages** to open the **Pages** panel.
   b) From the **Pages** panel options menu, select **New Parent**.
   c) In the **New Parent** dialog box, in the **Name** box, double-click and type *Left*
   d) In the **Based on Parent** drop-down list, select **A-Parent**. Select **OK**.

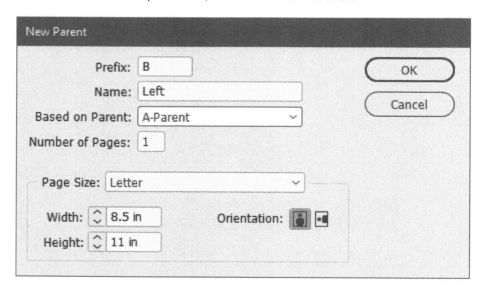

3. Add a repeating element to the new parent page **Left**.
   a) In the **Tools** panel, select the **Rectangle Frame** tool and drag a vertical rectangle on the left side of the parent.
   b) In the **Control** panel, verify that the **Reference Point** is set to center ⊞, and then specify the following values:

- X = *1.25*
- Y = *5.5*
- W = *2.5*
- H = *11*

c) Press **Enter**. Observe that the rectangle borders the left side of the page.

d) With the rectangle still selected, in the **Swatches** panel, select the **Fill** icon (do not select **Stroke**) and select the **Dark Green** swatch.

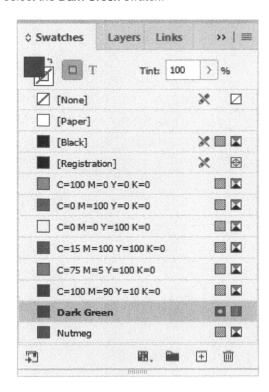

 **Note:** If the **Swatches** panel is not displayed, select **Window→Color→Swatches**.

## 4. Create another parent page.

a) From the **Pages** panel options menu, select **New Parent**.

b) In the **New Parent** dialog box, in the **Prefix** box, type *B*

c) In the **Name** box, double-click and type *Right*

d) In the **Based on Parent** box, verify that **(None)** is selected. Select **OK**.

e) If necessary, in the **Pages** panel, double-click the **B-Left** parent page to select it.

f) On parent page **B-Left**, switch to the **Selection** tool, select the green rectangle, and then press **Ctrl +C** to copy it.

g) Double-click the parent page **B-Right** and press **Ctrl+V** to paste the rectangle.

h) With the rectangle selected, in the **Control** panel, change the **X** value to **7.25** and press **Enter**.

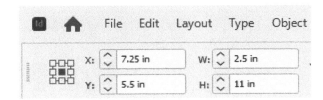

i) Verify that the rectangle borders the right side of the page.

j) In the **Control** panel, from the **Fill** drop-down menu, select **Nutmeg**.

5. Use the **Pages** panel to apply the new parent pages.

a) At the top of the **Pages** panel, right-click the parent page **B-Left** and select **Apply Parent to Pages**.

b) In the **Apply Parent** dialog box, in the **To Pages** box, type *2,4* and select OK.

c) In the **Pages** panel, right-click the parent page **B-Right** and select **Apply Parent to Pages**.

d) In the **Apply Parent** dialog box, in the **To Pages** box, type *3* and select OK.

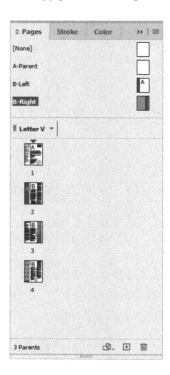

e) Double-click pages **2** through **4** to verify that the repeating element has been added.

f) Save the file in the **C:\092024Data\Managing Advanced Page Elements** folder as *My Nursery Newsletter.indd* and leave the file open.

# TOPIC B

## Change Text Layouts

Text-heavy documents require special formatting considerations. These typographic elements include justification, hyphenation, tracking, and kerning, just to name a few. Paying close attention to these details can make a difference in a document's aesthetic appeal.

### Hyphenation

*Hyphenation* is a format that determines whether or not text needs to be broken with a hyphen. You can set the minimum size of a word to be hyphenated, position the hyphen in a word, and determine whether to hyphenate capitalized words or not. You can also control the number of hyphens to be used in a paragraph. Hyphens can be inserted either manually or automatically.

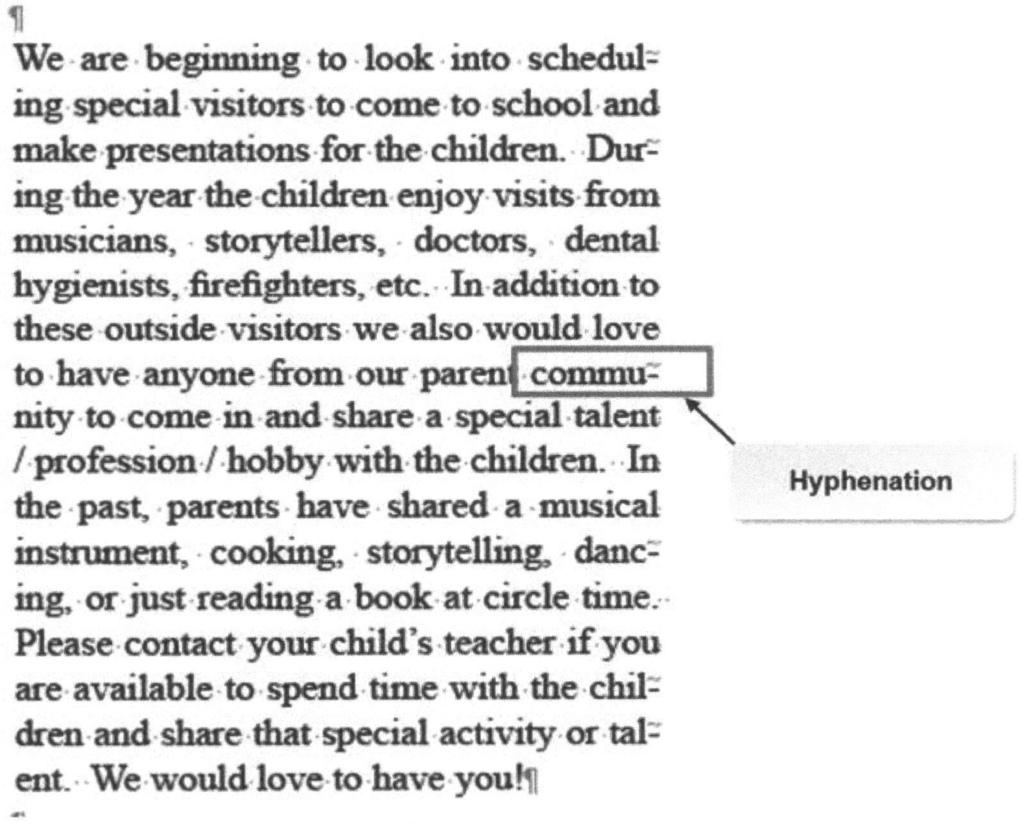

¶
We are beginning to look into schedul-
ing special visitors to come to school and
make presentations for the children. During the year the children enjoy visits from
musicians, storytellers, doctors, dental
hygienists, firefighters, etc. In addition to
these outside visitors we also would love
to have anyone from our parent community to come in and share a special talent
/ profession / hobby with the children. In
the past, parents have shared a musical
instrument, cooking, storytelling, danc-
ing, or just reading a book at circle time.
Please contact your child's teacher if you
are available to spend time with the children and share that special activity or talent. We would love to have you!¶

Hyphenation

*Figure 2-2: A hyphenation example.*

### Justification

*Justification* is a paragraph format that controls the spacing between words and letters in a document to ensure that text margins are evenly spread or appear evenly on the right, left, or both. It also controls the width of characters and the spacing between lines.

**Controls word and letter spacing**

For the month of November our activities will revolve around Thanksgiving. We will compare the first Thanksgiving and the Thanksgiving celebration of today. We'll talk about different kinds of food eaten for the feast and even do some baking ourselves. Most importantly, we'll focus on family and friends.

**Before justification**

For the month of November our activities will revolve around Thanksgiving. We will compare the first Thanksgiving and the Thanksgiving celebration of today. We'll talk about different kinds of food eaten for the feast and even do some baking ourselves. Most importantly, we'll focus on family and friends.

**After justification**

*Figure 2-3: An example of text before and after justification.*

## Keep Options

*Keep Options* is a feature that allows you to specify the number of lines that you want to retain in a paragraph or heading. The options in the **Keep Options** dialog box let you link adjacent lines of a paragraph and control paragraph breaks. This will prevent text from moving to another column, text frame, or page of a document.

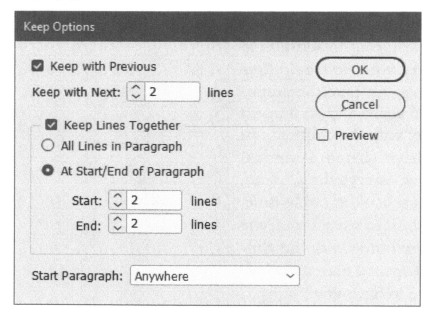

*Figure 2-4: Keep Options.*

There are different ways to control paragraph breaks using the options in the **Keep Options** dialog box.

| Option | Description |
| --- | --- |
| **Keep with Previous** | A check box that, when checked, keeps the first line of the current paragraph with the last line of the previous paragraph. |
| **Keep with Next** | A text box that allows you to keep up to five lines together with the last line of a paragraph. |

| Option | Description |
|---|---|
| **Keep Lines Together** | A check box that, when checked, allows you to keep lines of a paragraph together. The options in this section are enabled only when the check box is checked. |
| **Start Paragraph** | A drop-down menu that allows you to decide where the reunited paragraph must appear. The options in the drop-down menu include **Anywhere**, **In Next Column**, **In Next Frame**, **On Next Page**, **On Next Odd Page**, and **On Next Even Page**. |
| **Preview** | A check box that, when checked, allows you to see how the broken lines, such as orphans or widows, are retained with a paragraph. |

## Widows and Orphans

*Widows and orphans* are words or phrases that are left hanging, or those that are left behind in the text frame when a page or column break occurs. The first line of a paragraph separated by a column or page break is called the orphan line, and the last line of a paragraph that is pushed to a new column or page is called the widow line.

## Tracking and Kerning

*Tracking* is a character format that ensures equal spacing between characters in a selected word or paragraph. The spacing is measured in thousandths of an em. A positive tracking value increases the space between characters and a negative value decreases the space.

*Kerning* is a character format that adjusts space between two characters. It can be set either manually or automatically using metrics or optical kerning. *Metrics kerning* depends on *kern pairs* that contain details about spacing between different pairs of characters. *Optical kerning* spaces two characters based on their shapes and is useful when you are kerning two characters of different fonts. Kerning cannot be applied to more than one pair of characters at a time.

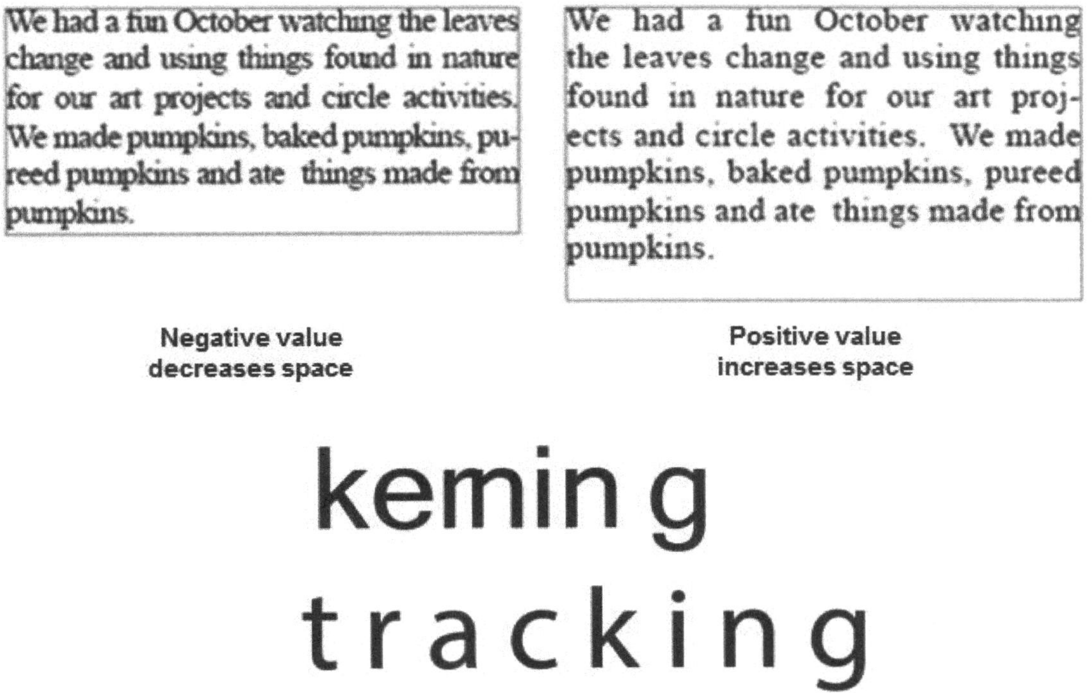

We had a fun October watching the leaves change and using things found in nature for our art projects and circle activities. We made pumpkins, baked pumpkins, pureed pumpkins and ate things made from pumpkins.

We had a fun October watching the leaves change and using things found in nature for our art projects and circle activities. We made pumpkins, baked pumpkins, pureed pumpkins and ate things made from pumpkins.

**Negative value decreases space**

**Positive value increases space**

# kernin g

# tracking

*Figure 2–5: An example of paragraph text with negative tracking and positive tracking values.*

## Split and Span Columns

InDesign allows you to make a paragraph span across multiple columns in a text frame. You can choose whether a paragraph spans all columns or a specified number of columns. When a paragraph spans across columns in a multicolumn text frame, any text before the spanning paragraph will be balanced between the columns that are spanned. You can also split a paragraph into multiple columns within the same text frame. The settings for spanning and splitting columns are available in the **Control** panel or the **Paragraph** panel.

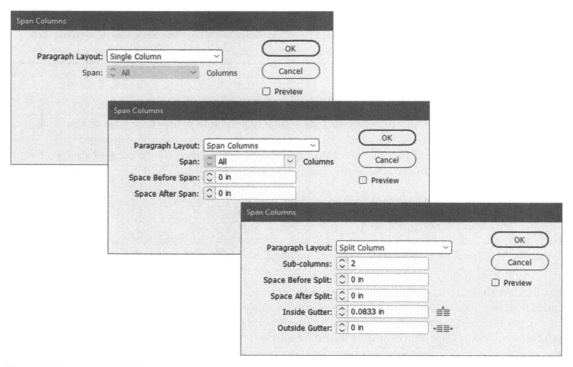

*Figure 2-6: Paragraph Layout options.*

## Sub-columns

In InDesign, you can split your text into sub-columns. This makes it convenient when you are creating an article or have a long list within your text. In order to create sub-columns, place your insertion point in a paragraph, and from the **Control** panel menu or **Paragraph** panel menu, select **Span Columns**. Then, from the **Paragraph Layout** menu, select **Split Columns**. As you configure the split, you can choose the number of sub-columns you want.

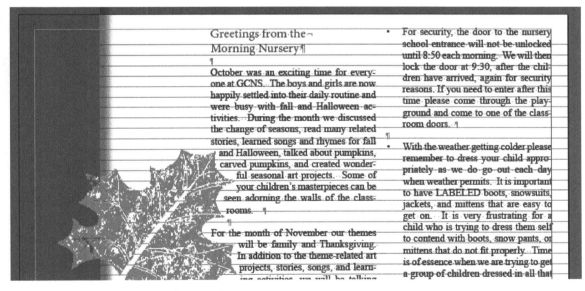

*Figure 2-7: Span Columns dialog box.*

## Document Baseline Grid

A document baseline grid is a non-printing grid for aligning columns of text. It appears on the screen as ruled notebook paper and covers the entire spread. It appears on every spread but can't be assigned to any master. It can be made to appear in front of or behind all guides, layers, and objects, but can't be assigned to any layer. Use **Grid Preferences** to set up a baseline grid for the entire document by selecting **Edit→Preferences→Grids**.

*Figure 2-8: Document baseline grid.*

## Scaling and Auto-Resize

*Scaling* proportionally resizes text in a text frame. When you scale text, the kerning, tracking, and leading values are automatically adjusted, avoiding distortion. To scale text, in the **Tools** panel, select the **Scale** tool.

 **Note:** If you do not see the **Scale** tool, right-click the **Free Transform tool** and select the **Scale** tool.

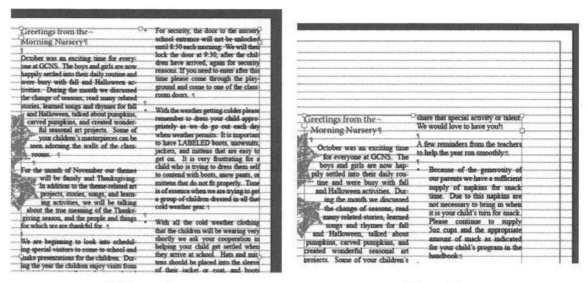

**Before scaling**　　　　　**After scaling**

*Figure 2–9: Scaling before and after.*

 Access the **Checklist** tile on your CHOICE Course screen for reference information and job aids on **How to Change Text Layouts.**

# ACTIVITY 2-2
## Changing Text Layouts

### Before You Begin
My Nursery Newsletter.indd is open.

### Scenario
You've created a layout for the nursery school newsletter. Since it is a fairly text-heavy document, you feel that it would benefit from some typographic enhancements.

---

1. Change to the **A-Parent** page and select the **Typography** workspace.
   a) In the **Pages** panel, select **A-Parent**.
   b) Navigate to page **1** and adjust the view setting to **100%**.
   c) On the **Application** bar, from the **Workspace** drop-down menu, select **Typography**.

2. Add kerning and tracking.
   a) Locate the newsletter heading "greene city nursery school" and with the **Type** tool, place the insertion point between the "r" and the "e" in "greene."
   b) In the **Control** panel, select the **Character Formatting Controls** button.

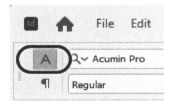

   c) In the **Control** panel, in the **Kerning** box, change the value to **-40**.

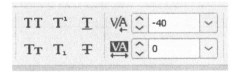

   d) In the "Dates to remember" section, highlight the text "Nov 1 Last tuition payment due."

   e) In the **Control** panel, in the **Tracking** box , change the value to **-42** and press **Enter**. Verify that the word "due" is no longer an orphan on its own line.

3. Add justification to the body text.
   a) Navigate to page **2** and adjust the view setting to fit the screen by pressing **Ctrl+0**.
   b) Starting with the word "October," highlight all the body text in the two columns.
   c) In the **Control** panel, select the **Paragraph Formatting Controls** button. ¶
   d) In the **Control** panel, select the **Justify with last line aligned left** button.

4. Keep first lines of a paragraph with the rest of the paragraph.

---

a) Highlight the last lines of text "We wish our GCNS families a very Happy Thanksgiving!" and select the **Paragraph** panel.

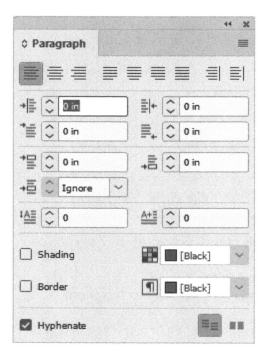

b) From the **Paragraph** panel options menu, select **Keep Options**.
c) In the **Keep Options** dialog box, check the **Keep Lines Together** check box and select **All Lines in Paragraph**.
d) In the **Start Paragraph** box, select **On Next Page**.
e) Select **OK**.
f) Verify that the text has been moved to the top of the next page in the document.

We·wish·our·GCNS·families·a·very·
Happy·Thanksgiving!·¶
¶

5. Save the file and keep it open.

# TOPIC C

# Create Transparency

Transparency is a useful tool in adding depth and visual interest to a layout. Drop shadows on text and graphics and the layering of objects with different opacity are just a few examples of how transparency can add to your document. In this topic, you will create transparency.

## Transparency

*Transparency* is a setting that allows you to adjust the opacity of an object. Transparency can be scaled from 0%, where the object is completely transparent, to 100% opacity, where the object is completely solid. Transparency can be applied to text and graphic objects.

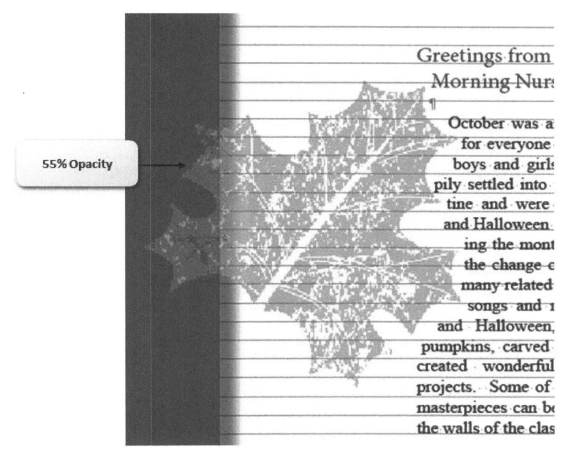

*Figure 2-10: Transparency example with leaf at 55% opacity.*

## The Effects Panel

The **Effects** panel allows you to determine the degree of opacity for an object, stroke, fill, and text. Using the components in this panel, you can specify how colors in transparent objects interact with objects behind them.

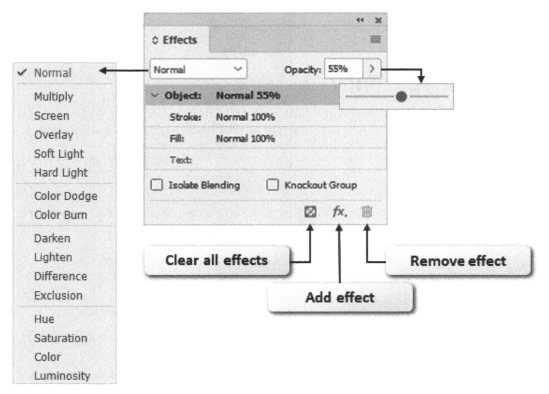

*Figure 2-11: The Effects panel.*

| Component | Description |
| --- | --- |
| **Blending Mode** | A drop-down menu that allows you to control the way colors of an object blend with the objects beneath it. |
| **Opacity** | A text box that is used to specify the opacity percentage. |
| **Isolate Blending** | A check box that, when checked, allows you to restrict blending to specific groups of objects and to prevent other objects from being affected. |
| **Knockout Group** | A check box that, when checked, allows you to block opacity and blending attributes of every object in the selected group. |
| **Clears all effects and makes object opaque** | A button that allows you to clear the effects of an object and makes the object opaque. |
| **Add an object effect to the selected target** | A button that allows you to add an object effect to the selected target. |
| **Removes effects from the selected target** | A button that allows you to remove effects from the selected target. |

## Transparency Effects

InDesign allows you to apply various preset transparency effects to objects.

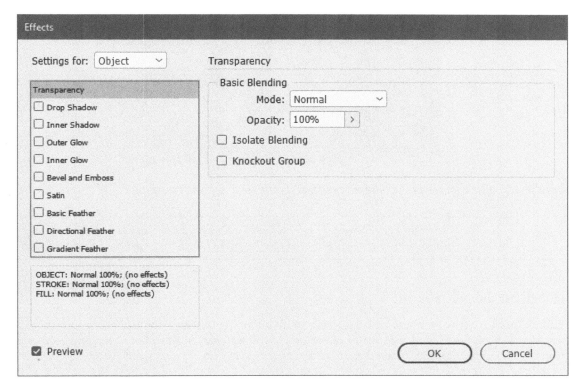

Figure 2-12: Transparency effects.

| Effect | Description |
| --- | --- |
| **Drop Shadow** | Adds a shadow behind objects, strokes, fills, or text. |
| **Inner Shadow** | Adds a shadow that falls just inside the edges of the object, stroke, fill, or text. |
| **Outer Glow** | Adds a glow that emanates from the outer edges of the object, stroke, fill, or text. |
| **Inner Glow** | Adds a glow that emanates from the inner edges of the object, stroke, fill, or text. |
| **Bevel and Emboss** | Adds various combinations of highlights and shadows to give text and images a three-dimensional appearance. |
| **Satin** | Adds interior shading to the object that resembles a satin finish. |
| **Basic Feather** | Softens the edges of an object over a specified distance. |
| **Directional Feather** | Softens edges of an object by fading the edges from specified directions. |
| **Gradient Feather** | Softens specific areas of an object by fading them so that they become transparent. |

The following figure shows an example of two transparency effects applied to a shape.

*Figure 2-13: An example of transparency effects applied to a colored shape.*

 **Note:** To learn more about using transparency with InDesign, check out the LearnTO **Make Realistic Drop Shadows** presentation from the **LearnTO** tile on the CHOICE Course screen.

## Blending Modes

Blending modes control the way colors blend with overlapping objects. You can group specific objects and check the **Isolate Blending** check box in the **Effects** panel to limit blending to specific objects. The blending modes offered in InDesign are the same ones available in Adobe® Photoshop® and create the same results.

**Access the Checklist tile on your CHOICE Course screen for reference information and job aids on How to Create Transparency.**

# ACTIVITY 2-3
## Creating Transparency

### Before You Begin

My Nursery Newsletter.indd is open.

### Scenario

The side panels you added to the newsletter parent pages look a little flat. You decide they would benefit from a drop shadow and a gradient effect.

1. Apply a drop shadow to the rectangles on the parent pages.

   a) In the **Pages** panel, double-click the parent page **B-Left**, select the **Selection** tool, and select the green rectangle.

   b) In the **Control** panel, select the **Effects** button *fx.* and select **Drop Shadow**.

   c) In the **Effects** dialog box, in the **Opacity** box, change the value to **50%** and in the **Angle** box, change the value to **180** and select **OK**.

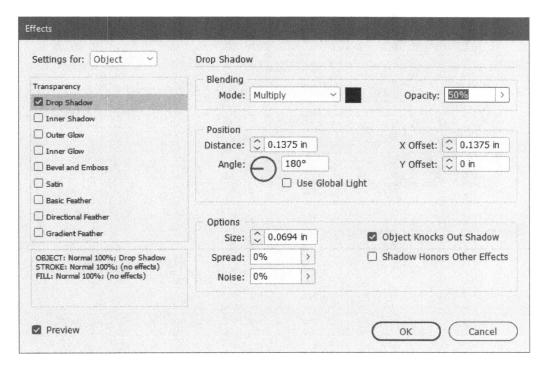

d) Examine the drop shadow effect on the left green rectangle.

e) Double-click the parent page **B-Right** and select the nutmeg rectangle. In the **Control** panel, select **Effects** and select **Drop Shadow**.

f) In the **Effects** dialog box, change the **Opacity** to **50** percent and change the **Angle** to **0**. Select **OK**.

2. **Apply a satin blending effect to the rectangles on the parent pages.**

a) With the nutmeg rectangle still selected, select **Effects** and select **Satin**.

b) In the dialog box, select **OK** to accept the default settings.

c) Double-click the parent page **B-Left** and select the green rectangle. Apply the **Satin** effect with the default settings and select **OK**.

d) In the **Pages** panel, double-click page **2** to display the page and verify that the effect has been applied.

3. Save the file and leave it open.

# TOPIC D

## Anchor Objects and Manage a Library

Anchored objects are considered best practice when it comes to including graphics in text. InDesign makes this a simple process that you'll find yourself using quite often. Libraries are also smart tools to take advantage of when creating documents. They help you organize the graphics, text, and pages you use most often. In this topic, you will anchor objects and manage a library.

### Anchored Objects

An *anchored object* is an object that is linked to a text frame. When you insert an anchored object, an anchor marker is displayed on that object. The anchored object can be a picture frame or a text frame. The anchored object can be positioned inside or outside a text frame. An object anchored to text will not need to be repositioned if the text reflows after being edited.

### Inline Graphics

An *inline graphic* is a graphic that appears along with its associated text. When text is edited or formatted, the inline graphic moves along with the text. You can position the inline graphic object below or above the line of text.

*Figure 2-14: Inline graphics example.*

### Libraries

A *library* is a file that is used to store objects that can be used later, either in the same document or in a different one. It stores objects such as rulers, guides, shapes, images, text, and pages. InDesign tracks the location of these objects on the hard drive. When a library object is deleted from the hard drive, it can't be accessed using the library.

 **Note:** Library files have the .indl file extension.

## The CC Libraries Panel

The **CC Libraries** panel allows you to manage items in a library. It displays library items and their names as thumbnail images. The **CC Libraries** panel contains options to search for, add, and delete library items. The **CC Libraries** panel options menu displays various commands that can be used to perform operations such as adding items to the library, placing items on a page, and updating and sorting library items.

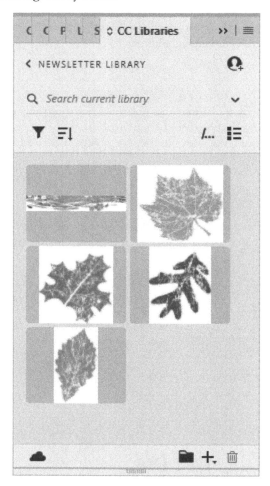

*Figure 2-15: The CC Libraries panel.*

## Adobe Capture

The Adobe Capture extension is accessed through the **Extract from Image** command and dialog box. It allows you to get color themes, shapes, and type. These can then be stored in the Create Cloud library. After capturing you can refine the assets using editing tools. The assets are saved to your active CC Library.

*Figure 2-16: The colors, shapes, and type in the selection are identified in the Extract from Image dialog box.*

 **Access the Checklist tile on your CHOICE Course screen for reference information and job aids on How to Anchor Objects and Manage a Library.**

# ACTIVITY 2–4
## Using Anchored Objects and the Library

### Data File

C:\092024Data\Managing Advanced Page Elements\images\turkey.jpg

### Before You Begin

My Nursery Newsletter.indd is open.

### Scenario

The text of the newsletter has some children's song lyrics that might benefit from an illustration anchored in the text. You would also like to set up a library file to organize the objects you may need to reuse in other documents for the nursery school.

1. Insert an anchored graphics frame.
   a) Navigate to page **3** and with the **Type** tool, place the insertion point after the text "The Turkey."
   b) From the **Menu** bar, select **Object→Anchored Object→Insert**.
   c) In the **Insert Anchored Object** dialog box, in the **Object Options** section, in the **Content** drop-down list, select **Graphic**. In the **Height** box, change the value to **0.5 in**.
   d) In the **Position** box, change the selection to **Inline or Above Line**.

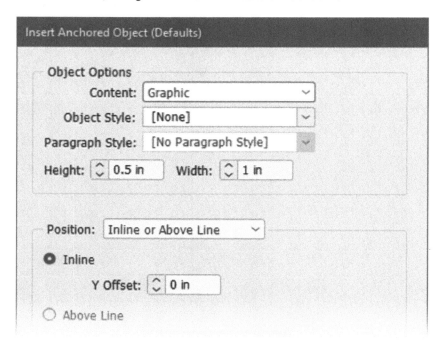

   e) Select **OK**.

2. Place a graphic into the anchored graphic frame.
   a) On the **Menu** bar, select **File→Place** and browse to the file **C:\092024Data\Managing Advanced Page Elements\images\turkey.jpg**.

b) Select the file and then select **Open**. You won't see the turkey yet.

c) Right-click the anchored graphic box and select **Fitting→Fit Content Proportionally**.

If you don't see the anchor symbol, select the **Selection** tool, then select just to the right of the turkey image.

3. Create a library.

   a) From the menu, select **File→New→Library**.

   b) In the **CC Libraries** dialog box, select **Yes**.

   c) In the **CC Libraries** panel, from the **My Library** drop-down, select **Create New Library**.

   d) In the **Library Name** box, type *Newsletter Library* and select **Create**.

4. Add images to the library.

   a) On page **1**, with the **Selection** tool, select the banner image and drag it into the **CC Libraries** panel.

b) Select all the leaf images on the remaining pages and drag them into the **CC Libraries** panel.

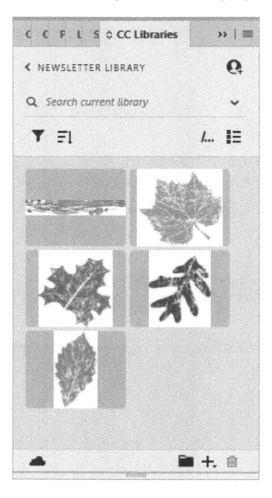

c) Collapse the **CC Libraries** panel.

5. Save and close the file.

# Summary

In this lesson, you used parent pages to create repeating objects in the document. You also used the typographic features such as justification, hyphenation, tracking, and kerning. Additionally, you learned how to use splitting and spanning columns, baseline grids, and scaling in documents.

**In your experience, were there times that you could have used parent pages when you created a document?**

**When would you want to make changes to the tracking or kerning of a paragraph?**

 **Note:** Check your CHOICE Course screen for opportunities to interact with your classmates, peers, and the larger CHOICE online community about the topics covered in this course or other topics you are interested in. From the Course screen you can also access available resources for a more continuous learning experience.

# 3 | Managing Styles

**Lesson Time: 45 minutes**

## Lesson Introduction

In Part 1 of this series, you learned how Adobe® InDesign® gives you the ability to create and save formatting for paragraphs, characters, and objects. It goes beyond these, of course. InDesign also lets you import styles from Microsoft® Word documents, build nested styles, apply styles in a sequence, as well as redefine and override styles. In this lesson, you will manage styles.

## Lesson Objectives

In this lesson, you will:

- Import styles from Microsoft Word documents.

- Apply styles in a sequence and manage overrides.

# TOPIC A

## Import Styles from Microsoft Word Documents

There will be times when you will be using content originally developed using Microsoft Word. This feature lets you preserve the formatting styles that were applied in Word and import them into InDesign. In this topic, you will import styles from Microsoft Word documents.

### The Microsoft Word Import Options Dialog Box

The **Microsoft Word Import Options** dialog box allows you to import different styles, such as paragraph, character, and table styles, from another document and format them in InDesign.

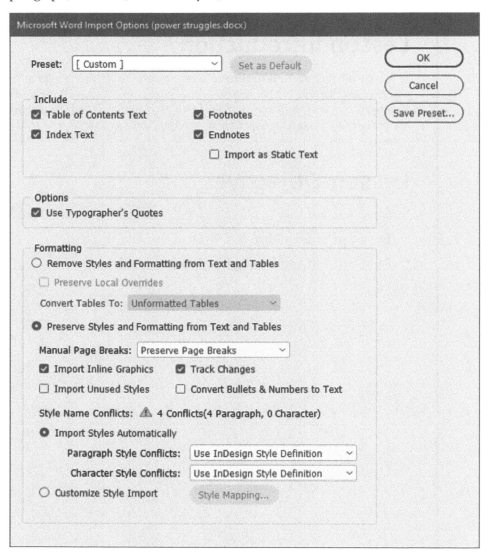

*Figure 3-1: The Microsoft Word Import Options dialog box.*

 **Note:** The warning in the figure was generated because a paragraph style being imported has the same name as an InDesign style, but the values differ between what InDesign has for the style and what the file being imported has for the style.

| Category | Description |
|---|---|
| **Preset** | A drop-down list that allows you to select a defined preset you want to apply. |
| **Include** | A section that contains options for importing the table of contents, indices, footnotes, and endnotes. |
| **Options** | A section that allows you to include left and right quotation marks and apostrophes instead of straight quotation marks and apostrophes in imported text. |
| **Formatting** | A section that allows you to format a document. Some options include the ability to remove formatting, preserve Word formatting, import styles automatically, resolve style conflicts, and customize the import. |
| **Save Preset** | A button that allows you to give a name to the defined preset and save the current settings. |

## Style Mapping

When you are importing a Word document that contains styles, and if the styles don't have the same attributes as InDesign styles that have the same name, you will need to map those styles. Select the **Customize Style Import** option, then use the **Style Mapping** dialog box to automatically rename conflicting styles, or select the InDesign style to use.

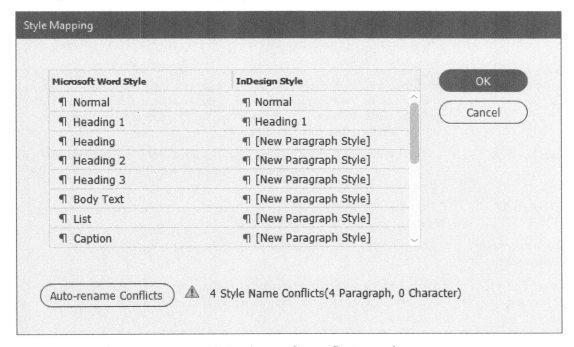

*Figure 3–2: Use the Style Mapping dialog box to fix conflicting style names.*

## The Load Styles Dialog Box

The **Load Styles** dialog box allows you to import paragraph and character styles from an InDesign document. There are various components that deal with the imported and existing styles of a document.

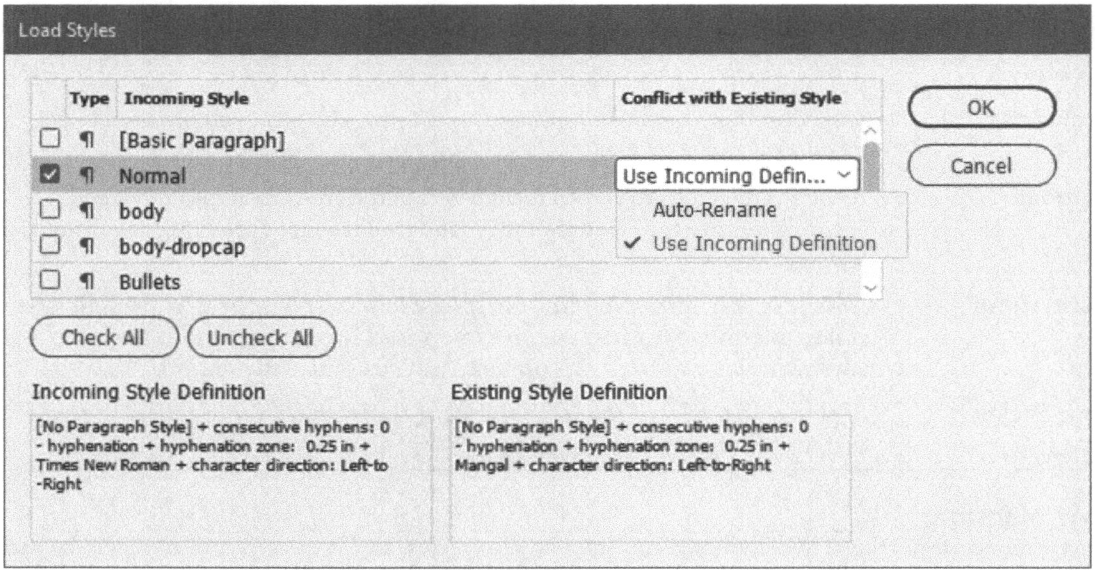

*Figure 3–3: The Load Styles dialog box.*

| Component | Description |
|-----------|-------------|
| **Incoming Style** | The options that display various paragraph and character styles of a document you want to import. |
| **Conflict with Existing Style** | The options that allow you to overwrite or rename the imported style if an existing style has the same name. The **Use Incoming Definition** option allows you to overwrite and apply the current style with the loaded style, and the **Auto-Rename** option enables you to rename the loaded style automatically in the current document. |
| **Check All** | A button that allows you to check all the styles under the **Incoming Styles** column and to display the corresponding styles under the **Conflict with Existing Style** column. |
| **Uncheck All** | A button that allows you to uncheck all the styles under the **Incoming Styles** column. |
| **Incoming Style Definition** | A section that allows you to view the attributes of incoming styles. |
| **Existing Style Definition** | For incoming styles that conflict with an existing style, this section allows you to view existing attributes of styles. If there is no conflicting style, this section is not shown. |

## Custom Style Mapping

Text styles (paragraph, character, table, and cell) or style groups can be mapped to different styles while linking. In the **Link Options** dialog box, accessed from the **Links** panel, enable **Define Custom Style Mapping** and then select **Settings**. Custom style mapping comes in handy, for example, when you want to use sans serif fonts for digital and serif fonts for print publications, or when you want to vary the text style between the horizontal and vertical layouts.

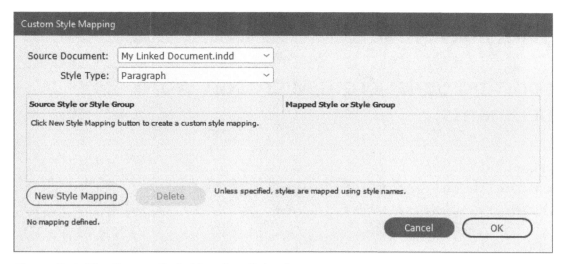

*Figure 3-4: The Custom Style Mapping dialog box.*

## Nested Styles

A *nested style* is a style that can be applied to specific ranges of text in a paragraph. Nested styles enable you to specify formatting to each character of text separately. They can be applied in different ways to a specified number of lines or sentences. Two or more nested styles can be specified to text. A sequence of nested styles, called nested style looping, can also be applied.

## GREP Styles

GREP is an advanced, pattern-based search technique. You can use GREP styles to apply a character style to text that conforms to the GREP expression you specify. For example, suppose you want to apply a character style to all the phone numbers in text. When you create a GREP style, you select the character style and specify the GREP expression. All paragraph text that matches the GREP expression is formatted with the character style.

 **Access the Checklist tile on your CHOICE Course screen for reference information and job aids on How to Import Styles from Microsoft Word Documents.**

# ACTIVITY 3-1
## Importing Styles from Microsoft Word Documents

### Data Files

C:\092024Data\Managing Styles\Nursery Newsletter Lesson 3.indd

C:\092024Data\Managing Styles\power struggles.docx

### Scenario

The latest newsletter for the Nursery School is close to being completed, but you've just received some last minute additions. You need to import the content from a Microsoft Word document.

1.  Optional step: Examine the style of the source Word document.

    a) In File Explorer, navigate to the folder **C:\092024Data\Managing Styles** and open **power struggles.docx** in Word.

     **Note:** If you do not have access to Microsoft Word, you can use the graphics in this step to identify the styles in the Word document.

    b) Place the cursor in the heading **Minimizing Power Struggles**.

    c) Right-click within the text and from the **mini-bar** context menu, select **Styles**. In the flyout menu, observe that the style is Heading 1. The font is set to Calibri Light 16 pt bold.

    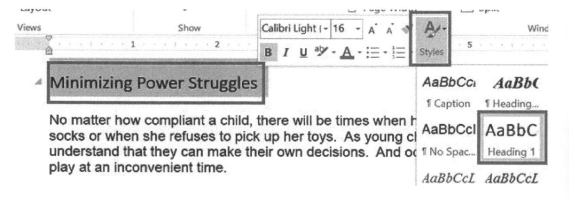

    d) Now right-click anywhere in the body text of the Word doc, and from the context menu, select **Styles**. Observe that the style is set to **Normal**.

    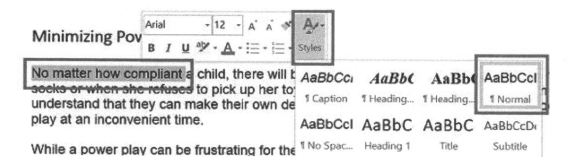

e) Close **power struggles.docx**.

2. Return to InDesign. From the folder **C:\092024Data\Managing Styles**, open **Nursery Newsletter Lesson 3.indd**.

> **Note:** If prompted to update links, select **Update Modified Links**.

3. On the **Application** bar, ensure that your workspace is set to **Typography**.

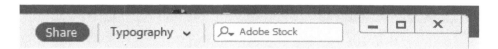

4. Import content from the Word document into the newsletter.
   a) Select the **Type** tool and on page **5**, press **Ctrl+H** to show the text frames, then click in the top-left text frame.
   b) From the menu, select **File→Place** and in the **Place** dialog box, navigate to **C:\092024Data \Managing Styles**, select **power struggles.docx**, and check the **Show Import Options** check box.
   c) Select **Open**.

5. Map the styles in the Word document to the styles in the InDesign document.
   a) In the **Microsoft Word Import Options (power struggles.doc)** dialog box, in the **Formatting** section, verify that the **Preserve Styles and Formatting from Text and Tables** option is selected.
   b) From the **Manual Page Breaks** drop-down list, select **Convert to Column Breaks**.
   c) Select the **Customize Style Import** option to enable the **Style Mapping** button. Select **Style Mapping**.
   d) In the **Style Mapping** dialog box, change the **Microsoft Word Style** of **Normal** to the **InDesign Style** of **Body**.
   e) In the **Style Mapping** dialog box, change the **Microsoft Word Style** of **Heading 1** to the **InDesign Style** of **Subheading**.

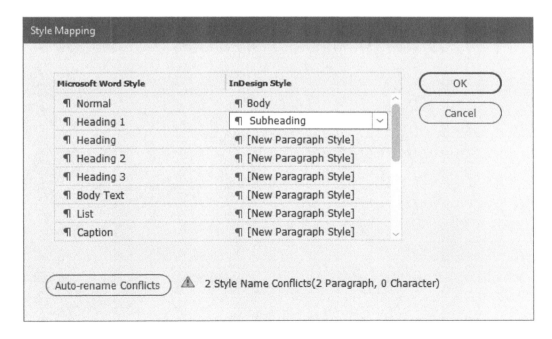

   f) Select **OK** twice.

g) If necessary, click in the left text box to import the text.

**Minimizing Power Struggles**

No matter how compliant a child, there will be times when he does not want to put on his socks or when she refuses to pick up her toys. As young children develop, they begin to understand that they can make their own decisions. And occasionally they make a power play at an inconvenient time.

While a power play can be frustrating for the adult who is trying to get the child to do something, it is a healthy part of children's social/emotional development. These incidents help

h) Observe the appearance of the text in InDesign. Compare it to the original Word doc.
i) In the InDesign **Tools** panel, if necessary, select the **Type** tool again.
j) Using the **Type** tool, place the insertion point in the heading "Minimizing Power Struggles."
k) In the **Paragraph Styles** panel, observe that **Heading 1** has been applied to the text.
l) Using the **Type** tool, place the insertion point anywhere in the body of the text.
m) In the **Paragraph Styles** panel, observe that **Body** has been applied to the text.

6. Save the file in the C:\092024Data\Managing Styles folder as *My Nursery Newsletter Lesson 3.indd* and leave it open.

# TOPIC B

# Manage Styles

The ability to define styles that are to be assigned in sequential order is a useful feature in InDesign. You can also override a style that's been applied to a paragraph. In this topic, you will apply styles in a sequence and manage overrides.

## Next Style

Next style is a formatting style that can be applied to text that follows the text to which a style is already applied. This style allows you to organize multiple paragraph styles in a sequence and apply them one after the other to subsequent paragraphs. Next styles are effective when a long document, such as a newspaper or magazine, needs to be formatted in a predefined order.

## Style Overrides

When a style is applied, text is formatted according to the defined style. *Style override* is a feature that is used when the format of a particular portion of text needs to be changed. When this feature is used, the new format applied to the selected portion of text overrides its existing style. The plus sign (+) next to the style name indicates that a style override is applied to the text.

## Object Style Options

Object styles are used to format frames and graphics much in the same way that character and paragraph styles are used to format text. There are a number of object style options from which to choose. The categories for object styles include:

*   Transparency
*   Drop Shadow
*   Inner Shadow
*   Outer Glow
*   Inner Glow
*   Bevel and Emboss
*   Satin
*   Basic Feather
*   Directional Feather
*   Gradient Feather

The settings for these categories can be turned on, turned off, or ignored via the **New Object Style** dialog box found in the **Object Styles** panel menu.

There are default object styles that are applied whenever new objects are created. These default object styles can be changed as desired in the **Object Styles** panel menu, via the **Default Graphics Frame Style** or the **Default Text Frame Style**.

## Style Redefinition

*Style redefining* is a feature that allows you to redefine character or paragraph style attributes in a document. Styles are a set of formats that allow you to create and apply text formatting. Using this style, changes to the formatting of the selected text can be applied so that they match the formatting of the text that was already changed.

## The Break Link to Style Command

Sometimes you want to copy a text frame and paste it into another document in InDesign. Unfortunately, when you do this, you also copy over any paragraph or text styles that were originally applied to the text and this can drastically change the formatting of the text in the new document.

Fortunately, in InDesign, you can use the **Break Link to Style** command, found both in the **Paragraph Styles** panel menu and the **Character Styles** panel menu. When you use the **Break Link to Style** command, the styles will be unapplied, which will remove any applied styles, but leave the formatting as is. Once this is done, you can copy and paste the text and retain the desired formatting in the new document.

 **Access the Checklist tile on your CHOICE Course screen for reference information and job aids on How to Manage Styles.**

# ACTIVITY 3–2
## Managing Styles

### Before You Begin

My Nursery Newsletter Lesson 3.indd is open.

### Scenario

The newsletters will all feature the lyrics to the song that the children will be learning that month. In an effort to streamline the formatting of the song title, artist, and lyrics, you decide to use the Next Style feature within Paragraph Styles. And while working on the formatting of the newsletter, you felt that repeatedly bolding the beginning of each calendar entry was tedious, so you will use the nested styles feature to save time.

You also decide to make adjustments to some hard-to-read lyrics.

1. Define the next style sequence for formatting the song on page 3.
   a) Navigate to page 3 and place the insertion point in a blank area of the right-most column.
   b) In the **Tools** panel, if necessary, select the **Type** tool.
   c) In the **Paragraph Styles** panel, double-click **Song Title**.
   d) In the **Paragraph Style Options** dialog box, in the **General** section, from the **Next Style** drop-down list, select **Artist** and select **OK**.
   e) In the **Paragraph Styles** panel, double-click **Artist**.
   f) In the **Paragraph Style Options** dialog box, in the **General** section, from the **Next Style** drop-down list, select **Lyrics** and select **OK**.
   g) In the **Paragraph Styles** panel, double-click **Lyrics**.
   h) In the **Paragraph Style Options** dialog box, in the **General** section, from the **Next Style** drop-down list, verify that **[Same style]** is selected and select **OK**.

2. Apply the styles in a sequence.
   a) On the nutmeg right panel of page 3, place the text insertion point in front of the word "Five." Hold **Shift** and click with the mouse pointer at the end of the last sentence after the text "Day."
   b) In the **Paragraph Styles** panel, right-click **Song Title** and select **Apply "Song Title" then Next Style**. Notice that they have different styles.

c) Click outside of the text frame to deselect the text. Verify that the styles have been applied in sequence.

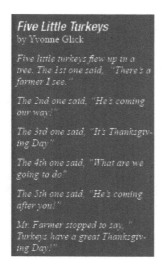

3. Create a **Character Style** to apply in the calendar section.

a) Navigate to page **1** and place the insertion point after the colon in "Nov 1:".

b) In the **Character Styles** panel, select the **Create new style** button. ⊞

c) Double-click **Character Style 1**. In the **Character Style Options** dialog box, in the **Style Name** box, type *Calendar Bold*

d) Select the **Basic Character Formats** tab in the left pane, and then from the **Font Family** drop-down list, select **Minion Variable Concept**.

 **Note:** If your list does not include this font, select a different font of your liking.

e) From the **Font Style** drop-down list, select **Bold SemiCondensed**.

f) From the **Size** drop-down list, select **11 pt,** and from the **Leading** drop-down list, select **Auto**.

g) In the left pane, select the **Character Color** tab, and then in the swatches list, select **Nutmeg**.

h) Select **OK**.

4. Create a nested style.

a) In the **Paragraph Styles** panel, double-click the **Calendar Item** style.

b) In the **Paragraph Style Options** dialog box, in the left pane, select the **Drop Caps and Nested Styles** tab.

c) In the **Nested Styles** section, select **New Nested Style**.

d) In the far left drop-down list, select **Calendar Bold** (the style you just created).

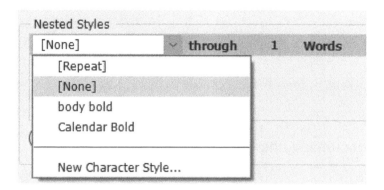

e) In the far right drop-down list, select **Words** and type a colon :

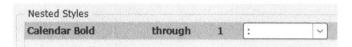

f) Select **OK**.
g) Under "Dates to remember", select all of the text in the column, then in the **Paragraph Styles** panel, select **Calendar Item**.
h) Unselect the selected text.
i) Verify that the month in each calendar entry is now bold.

5. Navigate to page 3 in the document.

6. Redefine the paragraph style applied to the song lyrics.
   a) Verify that the **Type** tool is selected.
   b) In the text frame containing the song, highlight the lines of text that contain the lyrics starting with "Five little turkeys flew up in a tree" and ending with "Thanksgiving Day."
   c) In the **Paragraph Styles** panel, select the **Lyrics** style.
   d) In the **Control** panel, from the **Font Family** drop-down list, select **Minion Variable Concept**.
   e) From the **Font Style** drop-down list, select **Display Medium**.
   f) In the **Font Size** drop-down list, select *10 pt*.
   g) In the **Paragraph Styles** panel, verify that the style **Lyrics** has a + (plus sign) next to it.
   h) From the **Paragraph Styles** panel options menu, select **Redefine Style**.
   i) Verify that the style **Lyrics** no longer has a + (plus sign) next to it.

7. Save and close the file.

# Summary

In this lesson, you imported styles from Microsoft Word documents, created nested styles, applied styles in a sequence, and redefined a style.

## When might you need to create a style based on an existing style?

## What are the advantages of creating and then redefining styles?

 **Note:** Check your CHOICE Course screen for opportunities to interact with your classmates, peers, and the larger CHOICE online community about the topics covered in this course or other topics you are interested in. From the Course screen you can also access available resources for a more continuous learning experience.

# 4 | Building Complex Paths

Lesson Time: 45 minutes

## Lesson Introduction

As part of the Adobe® Creative Cloud® Suite, InDesign® offers designers some of the same advanced graphics creation tools that are built into Illustrator® and Photoshop®. The ability to work with paths within InDesign is a convenient, time-saving feature. In this lesson, you will build complex paths.

## Lesson Objectives

In this lesson, you will:

- Create Bezier paths.
- Create clipping paths.
- Create compound paths.

# TOPIC A

## Create Bezier Paths

The **Pen** tool in InDesign is based on the industry standard and will seem familiar to InDesign users. While not a replacement for a full illustration program, it lets you build Bezier paths on the fly and make adjustments to ones imported from other programs such as Illustrator. In this topic, you will create Bezier paths.

### Bezier Paths

A *Bezier path* is a path that contains one or more straight or curved line segments. The start and end points of a segment are controlled by anchors. Two other points, called control points, determine the size and shape of the Bezier path. Regular shapes can be modified and converted into Bezier paths.

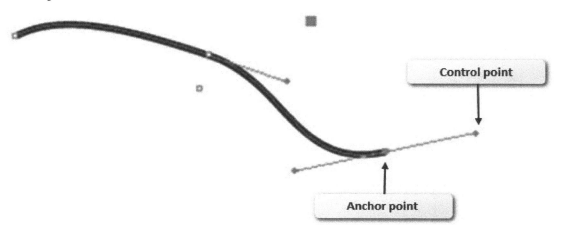

Figure 4-1: An example of a Bezier path showing the anchor points and control points.

### Bezier Drawing Tools

Bezier paths are created using the **Pen** or **Pencil** tool. InDesign provides tools that allow you to alter a Bezier path as well.

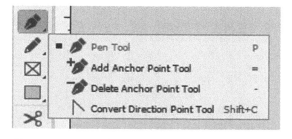
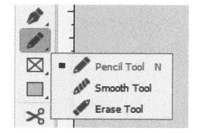

Figure 4-2: Tools to create Bezier paths.

| Tool | Used To |
| --- | --- |
| **Pen** | Draw straight and curved lines. |
| **Add Anchor Point** | Add anchor points to a path segment. |
| **Delete Anchor Point** | Delete an anchor point. |

| Tool | Used To |
|------|---------|
| **Convert Direction Point** | Convert a corner point to a smooth point and vice versa. |
| **Pencil** | Draw a free-form path. |
| **Smooth** | Smooth out the surface of a path segment by dragging the tool along the path. |
| **Erase** | Delete a path segment. |

## Text on a Path

Curved text can be created using paths. Text can flow along an open or a closed path. If text exceeds the path, it is hidden from view, which is indicated by a red plus sign (+) at the end of the path. However, you can thread the path to another and display the entire text either above or below the path. When a path's shape is altered, text takes the shape of the altered path. You can apply formatting attributes to the text, alter the stroke value of the path, and hide the path.

*Figure 4–3: An example of text on a path.*

## Type Outlines

A *type outline* is a path constructed by converting the outline of text to a path. The converted text is a set of compound paths that can be edited like a normal path. You can apply color strokes, gradients, or place a picture in the outline that spreads across the compound path. Anchor points can be dragged to modify the shape of the characters. Outlines can also be converted to text frames to hold text.

*Figure 4–4: An example of type converted to outlines.*

**Note:** To learn more about type outlines, check out the LearnTO **Use Type Outlines in a Layout** presentation from the **LearnTO** tile on the CHOICE Course screen.

 **Access the Checklist tile on your CHOICE Course screen for reference information and job aids on How to Create Bezier Paths.**

# ACTIVITY 4–1
## Creating Bezier Paths

## Data File

C:\092024Data\Building Complex Paths\Nursery Postcard.indd

## Scenario

As the publicity chair for Greene City Nursery School, it's your task to publicize the upcoming registration period. GCNS has a large mailing list so you feel a postcard is a good solution. After creating the layout, you decide to add a paint splash graphic behind some of the text.

1. Navigate to the folder **C:\092024Data\Building Complex Paths** and open the file **Nursery Postcard.indd**.

    **Note:** If prompted to update links, select **Update Modified Links**.

2. Draw a Bezier path.
   a) If necessary, navigate to page **1**.
   b) In the **Tools** panel, select the **Pen** tool.
   c) In the **Control** panel, from the **Fill** drop-down list, select **Dark Blue**.

      You may have to scroll to the bottom of the **Fill** list to see **Dark Blue**.
   d) In the **Stroke** drop-down list, verify that the selection is **[None]**.
   e) Draw a loose shape resembling a puddle of paint that completely covers the text "Open Registration Starts April 24th." Close the shape by clicking on the first anchor point when the mouse pointer turns into a pen with a circle. ✒ₒ
   f) From the menu, select **Object→Arrange→Send to Back**.

3. Make adjustments to the shape and the text.
   a) Switch to the **Selection** tool. If necessary, select the shape. In the **Control** panel, from the **Effects** drop-down list *fx*, select **Bevel and Emboss**.
   b) In the **Effects** dialog box, in the **Structure** section, from the **Style** drop-down menu, verify that **Inner Bevel** is selected.

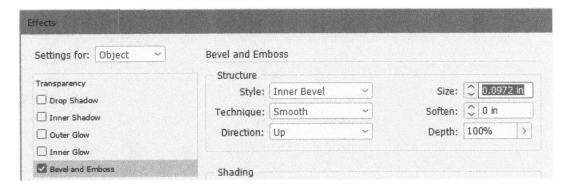

c) Select **OK**.

d) Using the **Type** tool, select the text **"Open Registration Starts April 24th!"**

e) In the **Swatches** panel, select the **[Paper]** swatch.

f) With the mouse pointer, click in the pasteboard area to deselect the text and verify the color.

4. Save the file in the C:\092024Data\Building Complex Paths folder as *My Nursery Postcard.indd* and then close the file.

# TOPIC B

## Create Clipping Paths

Clipping paths give you the ability to mask off areas of an image and allow other layers below to become visible. InDesign recognizes clipping paths saved in other programs like Photoshop and, on import, lets you preserve these paths. In this topic, you will create clipping paths.

### Clipping Paths

A *clipping path* is a path that is used to crop unwanted areas of an image. Though areas of the image outside the path are cropped, areas within the path are visible. The cropped portion is transparent, and other page elements are visible behind that cropped portion. A clipping path doesn't remove the area outside the path; it only makes it invisible. Clipping paths can be created both manually and automatically.

### The Clipping Path Dialog Box

The **Clipping Path** dialog box has options that are used to crop unwanted areas of an image.

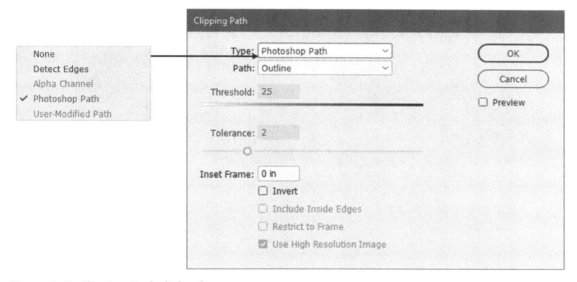

*Figure 4–5: Clipping Path dialog box.*

| Option | Description |
| --- | --- |
| **Type** | A drop-down list that allows you to select a path or channel for clipping paths. You can crop images using various clipping path types. |
| **Threshold** | A text box that is used to specify the darkest pixel value to define the resulting clipping path and create more transparent pixels. This can be done by increasing the range of lightness values added to the hidden area. |
| **Tolerance** | A text box that is used to specify a similar pixel lightness value to the threshold value to avoid unwanted bumps caused by stray pixels. |
| **Inset Frame** | A text box that is used to change the size of the resulting clipping path by defining threshold and tolerance values. |
| **Invert** | A check box that is used to switch between visible and hidden areas. |

| Option | Description |
| --- | --- |
| **Include Inside Edges** | A check box that is used to make areas transparent. |
| **Restrict to Frame** | A check box that is used to create a clipping path that stops at the visible edges of a graphic. |
| **Use High Resolution Image** | A check box that is used to calculate the transparent areas using the actual file for maximum precision. |
| **Preview** | A check box that shows a preview of the selected image with its clipping path. |

## Embedded Clipping Paths

An *embedded clipping path* is a clipping path on an image, which can be imported into InDesign. This path is created using image-editing software other than InDesign. It can be placed and edited in InDesign when it's saved in the TIFF or EPS format. An embedded clipping path can be automatically selected and manually edited; changes can be automatically previewed.

**Before Embedded
Clipping Path**　　　　**After Embedded
Clipping Path**

*Figure 4-6: An example of an image with an embedded clipping path.*

 **Access the Checklist tile on your CHOICE Course screen for reference information and job aids on How to Create Clipping Paths.**

# ACTIVITY 4–2
## Creating Clipping Paths

### Data File

C:\092024Data\Building Complex Paths\Sports Brochure Lesson 4.indd

### Scenario

You've added a photograph to the sports brochure but now you feel that it would look better if the background were taken out. You will use the clipping path feature to make this change.

1. Navigate to the folder **C:\092024Data\Building Complex Paths** and open the file **Sports Brochure Lesson 4.indd**.

    **Note:** If prompted to update links, select **Update Modified Links**.

2. Remove the gray background from the running shoe image on page 3 using an embedded clipping path.

   a) Navigate to page **3**.
   b) In the **Tools** panel, ensure the **Selection** tool is selected and select the running shoe image.

   c) From the menu, select **Object→Clipping Path→Options**.
   d) In the **Clipping Path** dialog box, from the **Type** drop-down list, select **Photoshop Path**.
   e) Verify that the path selected is **Outline**.
   f) Select **OK** to clip the gray background of the image.

g) With the **Selection** tool, click somewhere in the pasteboard area to deselect the clipped image.

h) Verify that the background is now invisible.

3. Save the file in the **C:\092024Data\Building Complex Paths** folder as *My Sports Brochure Lesson 4.indd* and close it.

# TOPIC C

## Create Compound Paths

InDesign, as in Illustrator, lets you combine multiple paths into compound paths to create unusual shapes with transparent areas. In this topic, you will create compound paths.

## Compound Paths

A *compound path* is a path that is obtained by combining two or more simple paths. When several paths are combined, the intersecting area of the paths creates a transparent hole that acts as an object. The fill color of the compound path is the fill color of the back-most object. The fill and stroke of the compound path are common to all the shapes that constitute the compound path. Gradient is applied as a whole to a compound path that is formed by paths that are not overlapping.

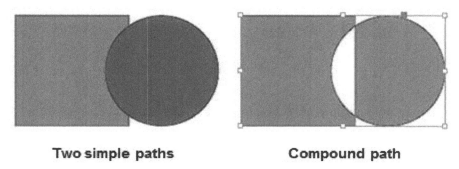

**Two simple paths**        **Compound path**

*Figure 4–7: An example of how two simple paths can be converted to a compound path.*

## The Pathfinder Panel

The **Pathfinder** panel is used to combine objects in different ways. It consists of four sections that help you in creating and modifying shapes. They are **Paths**, **Pathfinder**, **Convert Shape**, and **Convert Point**.

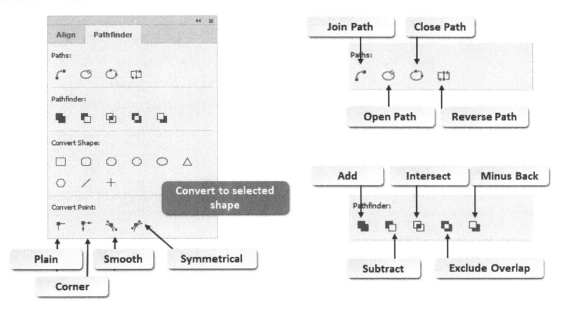

*Figure 4–8: The Pathfinder panel.*

## Paths

The **Pathfinder** panel contains four buttons pertaining to paths.

| Button | Used To |
| --- | --- |
| **Join Path** | Connect two end points of a path. |
| **Open Path** | Open a closed path. |
| **Close Path** | Close an open path. |
| **Reverse Path** | Change the direction of a path. |

## Pathfinder

The **Pathfinder** panel features five buttons that allow you to work with shapes.

| Button | Used To |
| --- | --- |
| **Add** | Create a compound shape where the intersecting lines are removed. |
| **Subtract** | Remove the shapes that are displayed in the front from the back-most shape. |
| **Intersect** | Remove areas that are not intersected by the selected shapes. |
| **Exclude Overlap** | Exclude the overlapping areas of two shapes. |
| **Minus Back** | Remove the back-most objects from the areas that intersect with the front-most object. |

## Convert Shape

The buttons in the **Convert Shape** section are used to convert the existing shape to a different shape. The available shapes include rectangle, rounded rectangle, beveled rectangle, inverse rounded rectangle, ellipse, triangle, polygon, and horizontal or vertical line.

## Convert Point

The **Convert Point** section offers the following options to convert a point.

| Button | Used To |
| --- | --- |
| **Plain** | Modify the selected points to have no direction points or lines. |
| **Corner** | Convert the selected points to have independent directional lines. |
| **Smooth** | Convert the selected points to form a continuous curve. |
| **Symmetrical** | Convert the selected points to smooth points that have directional lines of equal length. |

# Compound Shapes

Compound shapes are made up of simple paths, compound paths, text frames, text outlines, or any other shape. There are a number of options when determining the appearance of compound shapes, which can be accessed in the **Pathfinder** panel.

| Option | Description |
| --- | --- |
| **Add** | Creates a single shape using the outline of all the objects. |
| **Subtract** | The front object will punch holes in the object that lies farthest to the back. |

| Option | Description |
| --- | --- |
| **Intersect** | Creates a single shape by tracing the overlapping areas of all the objects. |
| **Exclude Overlap** | Creates a single shape from the areas of all the objects that do not overlap. |
| **Minus Back** | The back object will punch holes in the object that lies farthest to the front. |

Any attributes that the object farthest to the front holds will be applied to the compound shape, unless the front object is deleted by the action, in which case, the attributes of the back-most shape will be used. Text frames can be used in compound shapes, in which case the text will remain the same even when the shape changes.

 **Note:** To learn more about compound paths, check out the LearnTO **Use Compound Paths in a Custom Graphic** presentation from the **LearnTO** tile on the CHOICE Course screen.

 **Access the Checklist tile on your CHOICE Course screen for reference information and job aids on How to Create Compound Paths.**

# ACTIVITY 4-3
## Creating Compound Paths

### Data File

C:\092024Data\Building Complex Paths\Nursery Newsletter Lesson 4.indd

### Scenario

Now that you've added an article about discipline to the latest nursery school newsletter, you'd like to enhance the page with a simple illustration of a sheriff badge. You realize that the simplest and quickest way to create this graphic is by using compound paths.

1. Navigate to the folder **C:\092024Data\Building Complex Paths** and open the file **Nursery Newsletter Lesson 4.indd**.

    **Note:** If prompted to update links, select **Update Modified Links**.

2. Create a simple path shaped like a star.
   a) Navigate to page **5**.
   b) In the **Tools** panel, click and hold the **Rectangle Frame** tool ⊠ and then select the **Ellipse Frame** tool.

   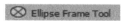

   c) With the mouse pointer, click once in the pasteboard area to the left of page 5.
   d) In the **Ellipse** dialog box, in the **Width** field, type *3*
   e) In the **Height** field, type *3* and select **OK**.
   f) In the **Control** panel, from the **Fill** drop-down list, select **Gold**.
   g) In the **Control** panel, from the **Stroke** drop-down list, select **[Black]**.

3. Create a simple circle shape to put on top of the gold circle.
   a) In the **Tools** panel, verify the **Ellipse Frame** tool ⊗ is selected.
   b) Click once in the pasteboard area next to the circle and in the **Ellipse** dialog box, enter the value *2.5* in the **Width** and **Height** fields, and then select **OK**.
   c) In the **Control** panel, from the **Fill** drop-down list, select **[Black]**.

d) Using the **Selection** tool, position the black circle so that it is centered on top of the gold circle.

 **Note:** Make sure the circles are completely in the pasteboard.

4. Create a compound path from the circle shapes.

a) With the **Selection** tool, click and drag a marquee box around the 2 circles so that they are both selected.

b) From the menu, select **Object→Paths→Make Compound Path**.

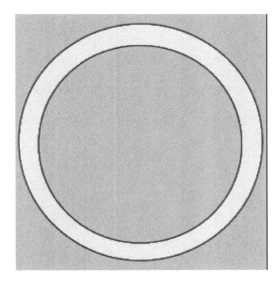

c) With the mouse pointer, click the pasteboard area to deselect the compound path in order to verify it.

5. Create a star to place on top of the circles

a) In the **Tools** panel, click and hold on the **Ellipse Frame** tool and then select the **Polygon Frame** tool.

b) With the mouse pointer, click once in the pasteboard area to the left of page 5.

c) In the **Polygon** dialog box, in the **Polygon Width** field, type *3*

d) In the **Polygon Height** field, type *3*

e) In the **Number of Sides** field, type *5*

f) In the **Star Inset** field, type *30* and select OK.

g) In the **Control** panel, from the **Fill** drop-down list, select **Gold**.

h) In the **Control** panel, from the **Stroke** drop-down list, select **Black**.

i) Using the **Selection** tool, center the star shape on top of the circles.

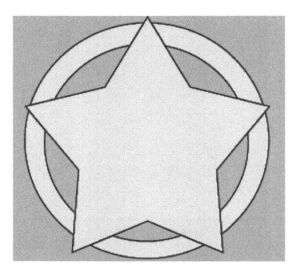

j) With the **Selection** tool, click somewhere in the pasteboard to deselect the star shape.

6. Add text to the sheriff badge graphic.

a) Select the **Type** tool, and then in the **Control** panel, from the **Font** drop-down menu, select **Times New Roman Bold**.

b) In the **Font Size** box, type *36*

c) With the **Type** tool, on the pasteboard, click and drag a text frame, then type *Sheriff*

d) Select the word **Sheriff**, and then in the **Swatches** panel, select **[Black]**.

e) Use the **Selection** tool to center the word "Sheriff" inside the cut-out star shape.

f) With the **Selection** tool, drag a marquee box around the compound shape and the text frame, and then from the **Menu** bar, select **Object→Group**.

g) In the **Control** panel, change the X and Y values to *4.75* and *1.75* respectively and press **Enter**.

7. Save the file in the C:\092024Data\Building Complex Paths folder as *My Nursery Newsletter Lesson 4.indd* and close the file.

# Summary

In this lesson, you examined how to create a Bezier path using pen and pencil tools. You also were able to use clipping paths to mask off areas of a graphic. Lastly, you saw how several simple paths can combine to create a compound path.

## How might you use compound paths in your layout?

## When would a clipping path come in handy?

 **Note:** Check your CHOICE Course screen for opportunities to interact with your classmates, peers, and the larger CHOICE online community about the topics covered in this course or other topics you are interested in. From the Course screen you can also access available resources for a more continuous learning experience.

# 5 Managing External Files and Creating Dynamic Documents

**Lesson Time: 1 hour**

## Lesson Introduction

As you build a document, you'll no doubt have to work with some external files. These may have layers or contain large amounts of data. Adobe® InDesign® allows you to manage the job of including content from these files efficiently. There are also features offered in Adobe InDesign that allow your documents to become dynamic. These include interactive behaviors, text variables, and automatic numbering, to name just a few. In this lesson, you will manage external files and create dynamic documents.

## Lesson Objectives

In this lesson, you will:

- Import external files and merge data.

- Create document sections.

- Insert text variables.

- Create interactive documents.

# TOPIC A

## Import External Files

When you need to include content from a source file that is built using layers, it's important for you to be able to preserve those layers for use in your InDesign document. When creating such things as form letters, envelopes, or postcards, you'll most likely be merging a data source that contains all this information. You can do this using the data merge feature. In this topic, you will import layered files and merge data.

### Layer Comps

*Layer comps* are different versions of an image stored in a file. Layer information of a particular version is stored in a layer comp and minor modifications to multiple layer comps are stored in a single PSD file. While the **Image Import Options** dialog box allows you to select a layer comp from a PSD file, the **Show Layers** list box displays a list of layers that belong to the selected layer comp.

### Image Import Options

When you import images and check the **Show Import Options** check box, the **Image Import Options** dialog box appears with a range of properties. When you import images, they are not automatically flattened. You can choose to import the layers as well.

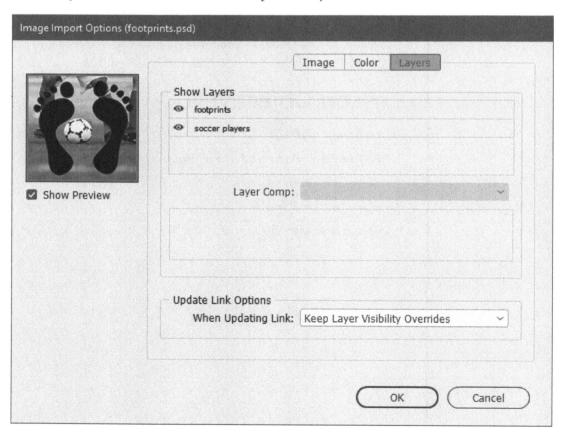

*Figure 5–1: The Image Import Options dialog box.*

| Section | Description |
|---------|-------------|
| **Image** | A tab with a drop-down menu allowing you to select any available clipping path in the target image. |
| **Color** | A tab that allows you to define the color profile and rendering intent. |
| **Layers** | A tab that displays the layers in the target file and allows you to toggle their visibility when imported into InDesign. |

# Data Merge

*Data merge* is a feature that is used to merge data from two files—a data source and a target. The file types that can be used as the data source are .txt and .csv files. Text that is unique to each document is stored in the data source file in the form of a record; text that is the same for all documents is stored in the target file. In addition to this, the target file contains placeholders for the data that will be populated later from the data source file. InDesign places data field values in the placeholders of the target document for each record and stores the record in a new file.

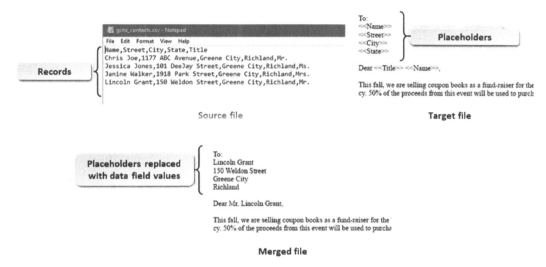

*Figure 5–2: Data merge.*

## The Data Merge Panel

The **Data Merge** panel is used to select the data source, add fields to the document, and create the data merge. You can enable the **Preview** check box to see example text from the data source as you are placing the fields. If **Preview** is not checked, then the field name within double chevrons is listed.

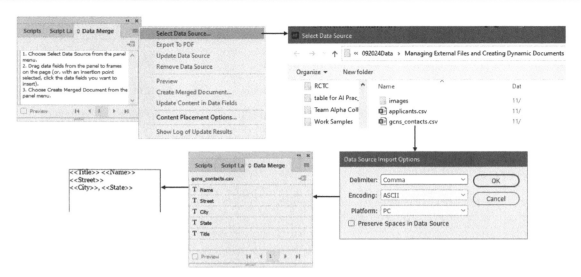

*Figure 5-3: Select a data source and options, then drag fields to place them in the document.*

## The Create Merged Document Dialog Box

Selecting **Create Merged Document** in the **Data Merge** panel (or selecting it from the panel menu), displays the **Create Merged Document** dialog box. In the **Records to Merge** section you can specify which records to use. In the **Records per Document Page** section, if the document contains only a single page, you can specify **Single Records** which places each record on a separate page or **Multiple Records** which would be used for something like printing a page of mailing labels.

The **Options** tab is used to specify image placement and how the image fits. It also includes options for removing blank lines if a field is empty and a limit to the number of pages per document.

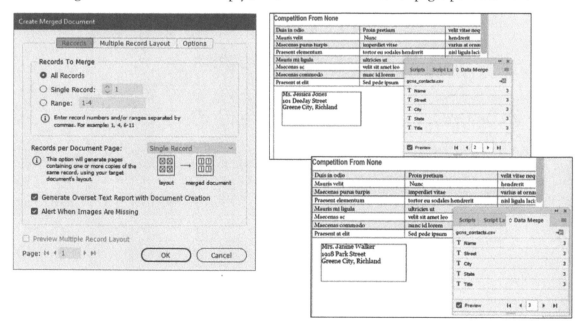

*Figure 5-4: A single record per document page and the Preview option.*

If **Multiple Records** is selected, the **Multiple Record Layout** tab can be used to set the **Margins** for each record, the arrangement of records, such as **Rows First** or **Columns First**, and the spacing between columns and rows. If there are multiple pages in the document, this feature is not available.

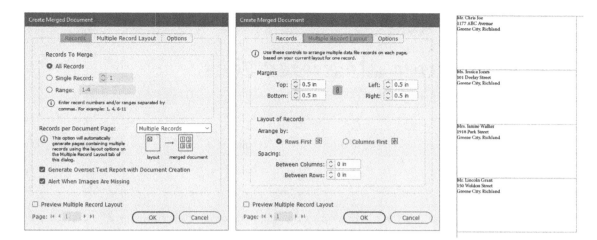

*Figure 5–5: Generate pages containing multiple records per page.*

## Data Merge Preview

When you select the option to place one record per page, the **Create Merged Document** dialog box does not have an option for previewing single records. The **Preview** option on the **Data Merge** panel is used to preview single records. For multiple records per page, you can select the **Preview Multiple Record Layout** in the **Create Merged Document** dialog box or use the **Preview** panel option.

 **Access the Checklist tile on your CHOICE Course screen for reference information and job aids on How to Import External Files.**

# ACTIVITY 5-1
## Importing External Layered Files

### Data File

C:\092024Data\Managing External Files and Creating Dynamic Documents\Sports Brochure Lesson 5a.indd

### Scenario

After looking over the brochure for My Footprint Sports, you realize that you forgot to include the footprint graphic from a Photoshop file. You will import the layered file into the brochure document.

1. Navigate to the folder **C:\092024Data\Managing External Files and Creating Dynamic Documents** and open the file **Sports Brochure Lesson 5a.indd**.

 Note: If prompted to update links, select **Update Modified Links**.

2. Create a rectangular frame to place the layered file.

   a) If necessary, navigate to page **3**.

   b) In the **Tools** panel, select the **Rectangle** tool and drag a square shape near the bottom of the page underneath the table.

   c) In the **Control** panel, type the following values:

   - X = *10.3*
   - Y = *9.2*
   - W = *2.5*
   - H = *2.5*

    Note: If the W or H value doesn't stay at 2.5, make sure the **Constrain proportions for width & height** button is not selected.

   d) From the **Control** panel, from the **Fill** drop-down list, select **None**.

e) Press **Enter**.

3. Import the layered file into the document.

a) From the menu, select **File→Place**.

b) In the **Place** dialog box, navigate to the **C:\092024Data\Managing External Files and Creating Dynamic Documents\images** folder and select **footprints.psd**. Verify that the **Show Import Options** box is checked. Select **Open**.

c) In the **Image Import Options (footprints.psd)** dialog box, verify that the **Show Preview** check box is checked.

Soccer players and footprints are both visible in the preview.

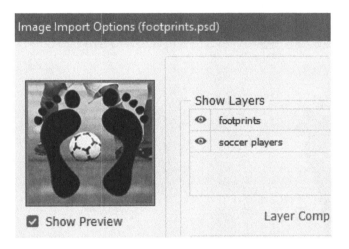

d) On the **Layers** tab, in the **Show Layers** section, select the **Visibility** icon of the **soccer players** layer to turn off its visibility.

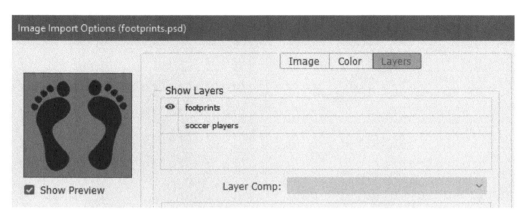

e) Verify that the soccer image is no longer behind the footprints image in the preview.

f) Select **OK**.

## Competition From None

| Duis in odio | Proin |
|---|---|
| Mauris velit | Nunc |
| Maecenas purus turpis | imperc |
| Praesent elementum | tortor |
| Mauris mi ligula | ultricie |
| Maecenas ac | velit si |
| Maecenas commodo | nunc i |
| Praesent at elit | Sed pe |

4. Save the file in the C:\092024Data\Managing External Files and Creating Dynamic Documents folder as *My Sports Brochure Lesson 5a.indd*

5. Close the file.

# TOPIC B

## Create Document Sections

Assembling a long document may require organizing it into sections. InDesign simplifies this with tools to help with creating sections and automatic numbering. In this topic, you will create document sections.

### Automatic Numbering

You can add a current page number marker to your pages to specify where a page number sits on a page and how it will look. Because a page number marker updates automatically, the page number it displays is always correct—even as you add, remove, or rearrange pages in the document. Page number markers can be formatted and styled as text.

### Document Sections

A *section* is a portion of a document that holds document items such as an index or a preface. Different styles of numbering, such as letters of the alphabet or Arabic or Roman numerals, can be used to number the sections. A document can be numbered section-wise, where numbering is restarted at each section. Page numbers can be prefixed to certain characters when numbering a section of a page. You can use either section page numbering or absolute page numbering when printing and navigating to different pages.

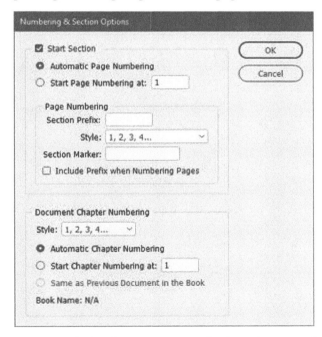

*Figure 5-6: Configure page numbering when creating a new section.*

 **Note:** If selected from the **Pages** panel options menu, this dialog box is labeled as **New Section**. It has the same options as shown above, which was selected from the **Layout→Numbering & Section Options** application menu.

## Section Page Numbering and Absolute Page Numbering

There are two ways to navigate to different pages: *section page numbering* and *absolute page numbering*. The section page numbering method allows you to access pages by using the page numbers specified for the section. For example, in S1-3, S1 is the section prefix and 3 is the page number.

In the absolute page numbering method, the pages are sequentially numbered. If section one has three pages, and you want to move to the third page in section two, enter the absolute page number as 6.

You can use absolute page numbering even when the section page numbering is used. When both methods are simultaneously used, you have to specify the absolute page number preceded by a plus sign ( + ).

 **Access the Checklist tile on your CHOICE Course screen for reference information and job aids on How to Create Document Sections.**

# ACTIVITY 5-2
## Creating Document Sections

### Data File

C:\092024Data\Managing External Files and Creating Dynamic Documents\Sports Brochure Lesson 5b.indd

### Scenario

The My Footprint Sports Brochure needs to be organized such that the first two pages are considered the introduction to the rest of the document. This will require the use of the sections feature.

1. Navigate to the folder **C:\092024Data\Managing External Files and Creating Dynamic Documents** and open the file **Sports Brochure Lesson 5b.indd**.

    **Note:** If prompted to update links, select **Update Modified Links**.

2. Define an introduction section.

   a) In the **Pages** panel, double-click page **2**.

   b) From the **Pages** panel options menu, select **Numbering & Section Options**.

   Alternatively, you can select **Layout→Numbering & Section Options** in which case the dialog box is named **Numbering & Section Options** rather than **New Section**.

   c) In the **New Section** dialog box, in the **Start Section** section, select the **Start Page Numbering at** option and verify that the value is **1**.

   d) In the **Page Numbering** section, in the **Section Prefix** box, type *B*

   e) From the **Style** drop-down menu, select **i, ii, iii, iv...**

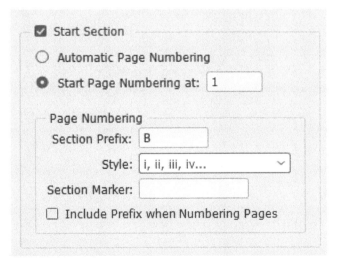

f) Select **OK**.

>  **Note:** In the **Pages** panel, the start of a section is indicated by a black triangle icon above the page thumbnail. Hovering over the triangle icon will give information about that section and double-clicking it will open up the **Numbering & Section Options** dialog box.

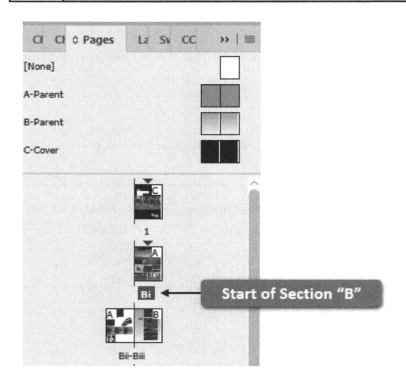

3. Define the end of the introduction section.

   a) In the **Pages** panel, double-click page **Biii**.

   b) In the **Pages** panel options menu, select **Numbering & Section Options**.
   c) In the **Start Section** section, select the **Start Page Numbering at** option, and verify that the value is **1**.

d) In the **Page Numbering** section, in the **Section Prefix** box, type *C* and select OK.

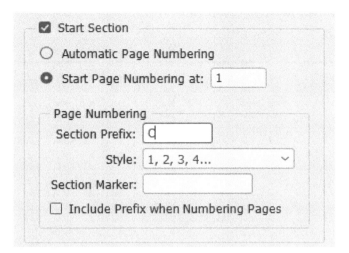

e) In the **Pages** panel, verify that the page thumbnails are reorganized into labeled sections.

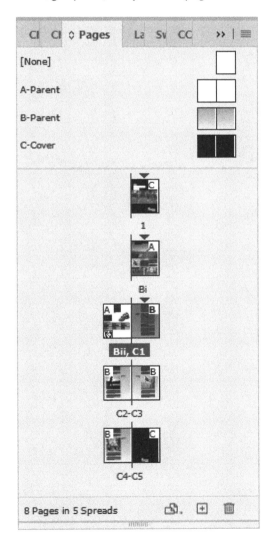

4. Save the file in the C:\092024Data\Managing External Files and Creating Dynamic Documents folder as *My Sports Brochure Lesson 5b.indd*

5. Close the file.

# TOPIC C

## Insert Text Variables

Text variables are items that you can place in your document that change based on the context. They're very useful and InDesign has a range for you to take advantage of. In this topic, you will insert text variables.

## Text Variables

A text variable is an item that stores text values that can be changed dynamically according to the context in a document. There are different kinds of text variables.

| Text Variable | Used To |
|---|---|
| **Chapter Number** | Insert chapter numbers. |
| **Creation Date** | Insert the date the document was created. |
| **File Name** | Insert the name of the current file. |
| **Image Name** | Insert the name of the current image. |
| **Last Page Number** | Add the total number of pages in a document. |
| **Modification Date** | Insert the date the document was last modified. |
| **Output Date** | Insert the date on which the document starts as a print job or is exported as a PDF file. |
| **Running Header** | Insert the first or last occurrence of the text on the page to which the specified style is applied. |

## The Text Variables Dialog Box

The **Text Variables** dialog box has options that allow you to perform various functions with variables.

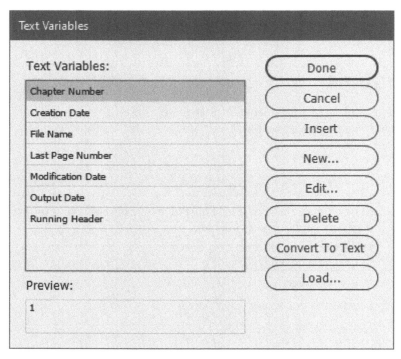

*Figure 5-7: The Text Variables dialog box.*

The following lists the functions you can perform with **Text Variables**.

| Component | Description |
| --- | --- |
| **Text Variables** | A list box that allows you to select the default or custom variable in order to edit it. |
| **Insert** | A button that enables you to insert the default or custom variable. |
| **New** | A button that allows you to create a text variable. |
| **Edit** | A button that allows you to edit the default or custom variable. |
| **Delete** | A button that allows you to delete the default variable or custom variable. |
| **Convert To Text** | A button that allows you to convert a text variable to text. |
| **Load** | A button that enables you to overwrite an existing variable with the loaded variable, and to apply its new attributes to the text in the current document. |
| **Preview** | A section that allows you to preview a text variable in a document when you select, create, or edit variables. |

# Glyphs

Glyphs are special shapes that exist in fonts. They can be used when you want to enter text in a foreign language, when you want to enter some alternative form for a letter, or when you want to use special symbols. Glyphs can be accessed via the **Glyphs** panel. When you first access the **Glyphs** panel, you will automatically be shown glyphs that match the font where your cursor is positioned. However, you can easily view glyphs in other fonts and type styles. In the **Glyphs** panel, you can access:

- A subset of glyphs
- Tooltip
- Font list

• Font styles

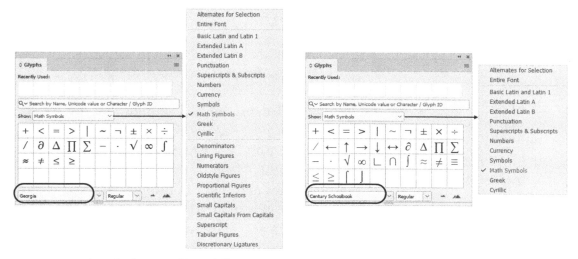

*Figure 5-8: The Glyphs panel has different options depending on which font is selected.*

## Hidden Characters

Hidden characters are those characters that don't print, such as the characters that represent spaces, hard returns, tabs, and index markers. These hidden characters can be viewed only in the story editor window and in document view. However, you can choose to view the hidden characters by using the **Show Hidden Characters** command from the **Type** menu. Just be sure to turn off the **Preview** mode in order to view the hidden characters.

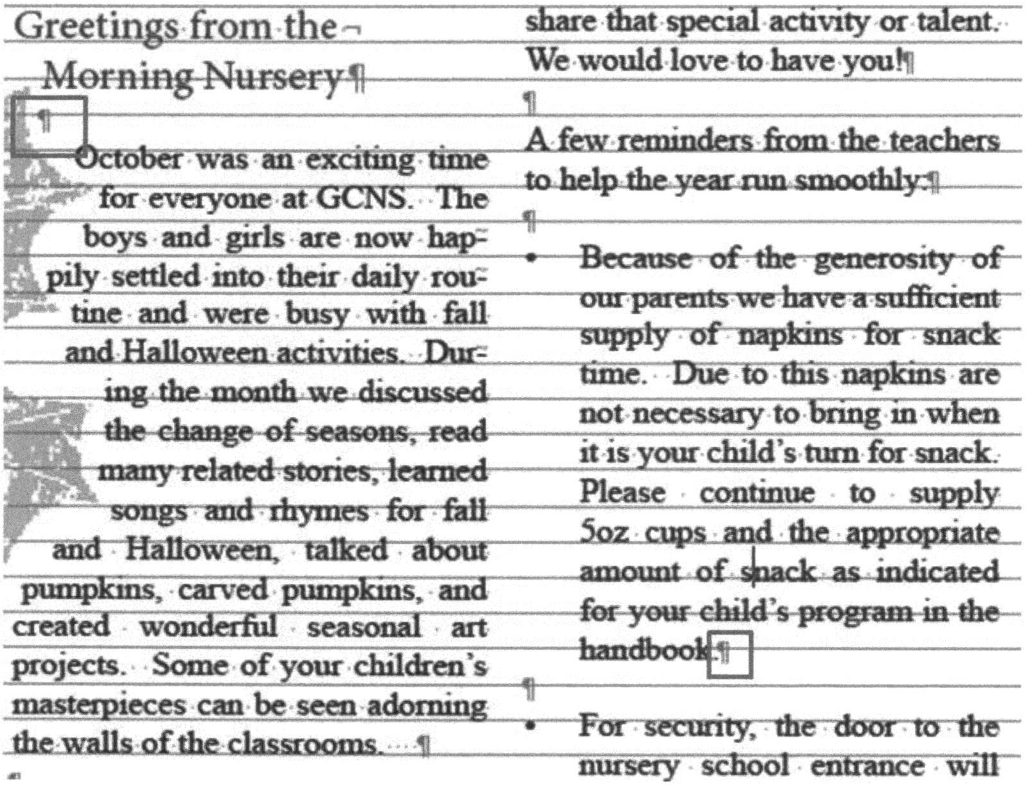

Greetings from the ¬
Morning Nursery ¶

October was an exciting time for everyone at GCNS. The boys and girls are now happily settled into their daily routine and were busy with fall and Halloween activities. During the month we discussed the change of seasons, read many related stories, learned songs and rhymes for fall and Halloween, talked about pumpkins, carved pumpkins, and created wonderful seasonal art projects. Some of your children's masterpieces can be seen adorning the walls of the classrooms. ··· ¶

share that special activity or talent. We would love to have you! ¶

¶

A few reminders from the teachers to help the year run smoothly: ¶

¶

• Because of the generosity of our parents we have a sufficient supply of napkins for snack time. Due to this napkins are not necessary to bring in when it is your child's turn for snack. Please continue to supply 5oz cups and the appropriate amount of snack as indicated for your child's program in the handbook. ¶

¶

• For security, the door to the nursery school entrance will

*Figure 5-9: Hidden Characters example.*

> Access the Checklist tile on your CHOICE Course screen for reference information and job aids on **How to Insert Text Variables.**

# ACTIVITY 5-3
## Inserting Text Variables

### Data File

C:\092024Data\Managing External Files and Creating Dynamic Documents\Nursery Newsletter Lesson 5.indd

### Scenario

At a recent Greene City Nursery School board meeting, it was suggested that page numbering for the newsletter should also include the total number of pages. You're pretty sure that this will be easy to accomplish using text variables.

---

1. Navigate to the folder **C:\092024Data\Managing External Files and Creating Dynamic Documents** and open the file **Nursery Newsletter Lesson 5.indd.**

    **Note:** If prompted to update links, select **Update Modified Links.**

2. Insert page numbering on a parent page.
   a) In the **Pages** panel, double-click the page **A-Parent** to display it.
   b) With the **Type** tool, drag a text frame in the bottom-right corner of the page, aligned with the right and bottom margin.
   c) In the **Swatches** panel, select **[Black].**
   d) In the **Control** panel, in the **Font Size** box, change the value to *9*
   e) Type the word *Page* and then press the **Spacebar.**
   f) From the menu, select **Type→Insert Special Character→Markers→Current Page Number.** and press the **Spacebar.**

3. Define a text variable.
   a) From the menu, select **Type→Text Variables→Define.**
   b) In the **Text Variables** dialog box, in the left pane, select **Last Page Number** and select **Edit.**
   c) In the **Edit Text Variable** dialog box, in the **Text Before** box, type *of* and then press the **Spacebar.**
   d) Select **OK.**

4. Insert a text variable after the current page.
   a) In the **Text Variables** dialog box, select **Insert.** Verify that the last page number variable "of 1" has been inserted into the text frame after the current page number "A."

   b) Select **Done.**

   c) In the **Control** panel, select **Paragraph Setting Controls,** then select the **Align Right** button. Position the text frame so that it aligns with the right and bottom margins.

---

d) In the **Pages** panel, double-click page **1** and verify that the current page and last page numbers display.

e) Scroll through the document and notice that pages **2** and **4** have the new page numbering, but pages **3** and **5** don't have page numbering.

5. **Why do some pages have the new numbering and some don't?**

6. **Apply page numbering to the other parent page.**

a) Double-click the parent page **A-Parent** and select the text frame containing the text variables "Page A of 1." Press **Ctrl+C** to copy the text frame.

b) Double-click the parent page **B-Right**. Press **Ctrl+V** to paste the text frame in the page.

c) In the **Paragraph** panel, select the **Align Left** button.

d) In the **Control** panel, in the X and Y fields, change the values to *0.85* and *10.65* respectively, and press **Enter**.

 **Note:** If your page number text frame is off the page or not quite where you like it, use the **Selection** tool to reposition it in the lower-left corner of the page.

e) In the **Pages** panel, double-click pages **3** and **5** to verify that they have page numbering applied to them.

7. **Save the file in the C:\092024Data\Managing External Files and Creating Dynamic Documents folder as** *My Nursery Newsletter Lesson 5.indd* **and close the file.**

# TOPIC D

# Create Interactive Documents

In this day and age of fast-moving technology, you can't always get away with creating static documents to engage a reader. InDesign offers a number of ways to insert interactive features like buttons, animations, sound, and videos as you build a document. In this topic, you will create interactive documents.

## Interactive Documents

An *interactive document* is a document that contains various interactive elements. You can create an interactive document using a combination of media such as video, animation, text, still images, and more. InDesign has continued to advance its ability to create documents that go beyond print. The various panels and tools in InDesign have made it possible for designers to create interactive workflow and digital publishing.

### Panels for Creating Interactive Documents

The **Digital Publishing** workspace in the application bar displays a range of panels that provide quick access to commonly used tools and features for creating interactive documents.

| Component | Description |
| --- | --- |
| **Animation** | A panel that lets you assign a motion preset to any page item, allowing you to create animations quickly. |
| **Timing** | A panel that allows you to determine the order of objects for animation instead of following the default order. Based on the page event that was assigned to each animation in the **Animation** panel, the list of animations on the current spread will be filtered. The **Play Together** button in the panel allows you to play multiple animated objects at one time. |
| **Media** | A panel that allows you to preview SWF, FLV, and MP3 files directly in InDesign without having to switch to another application. |
| **Object States** | A panel that allows you to not only support the creation of remote rollovers for interactive documents, but also create multiple versions of an object. Any number of versions or states can be created for an object. |
| **Buttons and Forms** | A panel that allows you to add form elements such as text fields, radio buttons, check boxes, list boxes, and signature fields to your document. |
| **Hyperlinks** | A panel that can be used to create links to jump to other locations in the same document, to other documents, or to websites. |
| **Liquid Layout** | A panel that lets you efficiently design your content for multiple page sizes, orientations, or aspect ratios. |

## The Presentation Mode

The *Presentation mode* enables you to preview an active document as a presentation. In **Presentation** mode, the document window switches to the **Full screen** mode, hiding the application menu and panels. It's an excellent choice to show a client what the document will look like without menus, panels, and other programs to distract the eye. Just realize that a document cannot be edited in this mode.

To enter **Presentation** mode, select **View→Screen Mode→Presentation**, or press **Shift+W**. To exit, press **Shift+W** or **Esc**.

You can move forward or backward through the document, one spread at a time, using the arrow keys. In this mode, the spread fits to the window proportionally and the extra space around the spread, if any, will be displayed in gray by default.

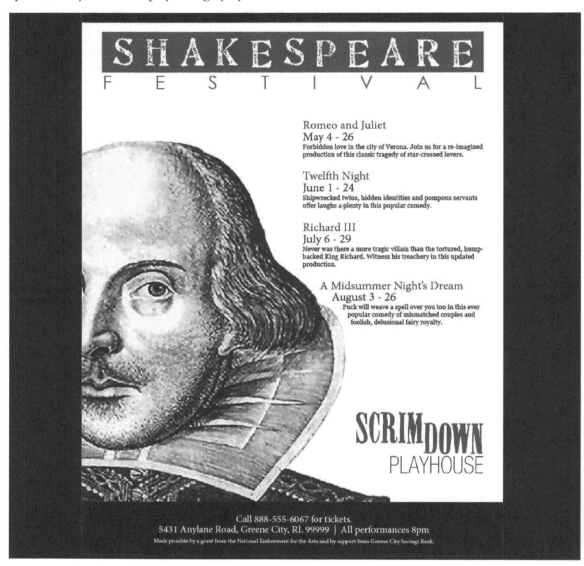

*Figure 5-10: Presentation mode example.*

 **Note:** The background color of the **Presentation** mode screen can be changed to white or black by pressing the **W** or **B** keys. To change it back to default gray, press the **G** key.

## The Animation Panel

Motion presets are pre-made animations that you can apply to objects quickly. Use the **Animation** panel to apply motion presets and change animation settings such as duration and speed. The **Animation** panel also lets you specify when an animated object plays. You can save motion presets you create and use them in other InDesign documents.

*Figure 5-11: The Animation panel.*

 **Note:** For more information on animation, see the article "Animation" at **https://helpx.adobe.com/indesign/using/animation.html**.

## The Timing Panel

Use the **Timing** panel to change the order of when animated objects play. The **Timing** panel lists the animations on the current spread based on the page event assigned to each animation. For example, you can change one set of animations that occur when the page is loaded, and then change another set of animations that occur when the page is clicked. Animated objects are listed in the order they were created. Animations listed for the **Page Load** event occur sequentially by default. Animations listed for the **Page Click** event are played in sequence each time the page is clicked.

*Figure 5-12: The Timing panel.*

# Page Transitions

Page transitions are used to create a visual decorative effect such as a dissolve or wipe in the interactive document when the file is exported in the PDF or SWF format. In InDesign, you can apply page transitions directly to individual pages or to all spreads in a single click. You cannot apply transitions to different pages within the same spread or to parent pages.

# Object Export Options

Object export options are used to specify export parameters required when you export to different formats such as EPUB, HTML, or tagged PDFs. Object export options are applied to text frames and graphic frames, as well as groups. Object export options are specified to individual objects or groups and can override the global export settings. Select **Object→Object Export Options**.

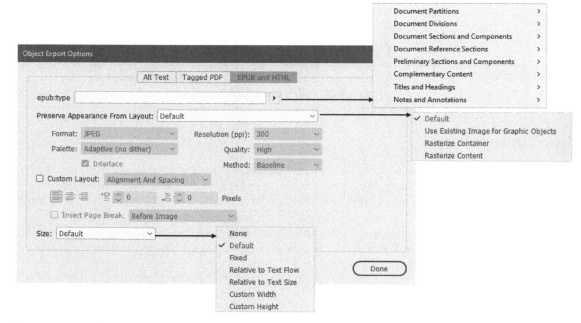

*Figure 5-13: The Object Export Options dialog box.*

# Style Export Tags

Use **Export Tagging** to define how text with InDesign styles is marked up in HTML, EPUB, or tagged PDF output. You can also specify CSS class names to add to the exported content. In EPUB/HTML export, CSS classes can be used to differentiate between slight variations in styling. Class names are required if you are using the option to **Include Style Definitions** and the tags are mapped to the basic styles such as p, h1, and h2; class names are then used to generate style definitions. You cannot preview **Export Tagging** within the InDesign layout, as it only impacts the exported EPUB, HTML, or PDF file. **Edit All Export Tags** lets you efficiently view and modify the mappings in a single dialog box.

# The EPUB Interactivity Preview Panel

The **EPUB Interactivity Preview** panel lets you review the animations in a thumbnail view within the panel so that you don't have to leave the InDesign application. It also allows you to play the animation defined in the document.

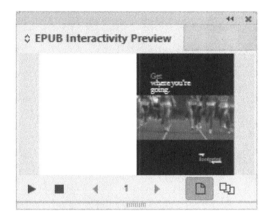

*Figure 5–14: The EPUB Interactivity Preview panel.*

# The Media Panel

Movies and sound clips you add to a document can be played when the document is exported to Adobe PDF® . Use the **Media** panel (select **Window→Interactive→Media**) to preview a media file and to change settings such as **Play On Page Load**, **Loop**, and sound. You can use the standard icon as the **Poster** for an audio media file, or use an image to represent the audio content. In the following figure, the audio is for music inspired by an airshow, and the **Poster** is a photo of the contrails the planes left in the sky from the airshow.

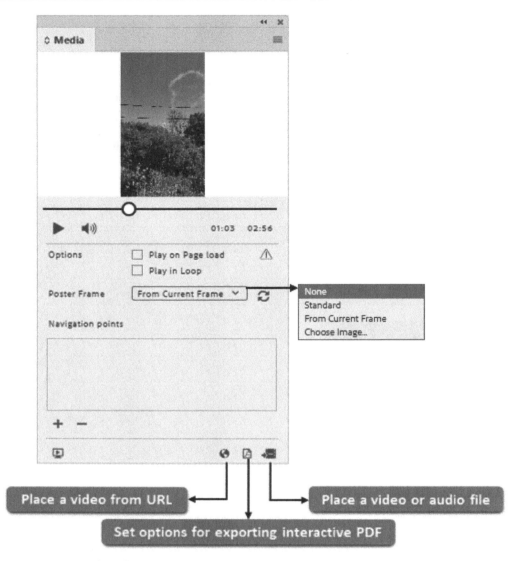

*Figure 5-15: A video clip with sound.*

For a video, you can set the **Poster** to the standard icon. You can also play through the video and select a frame, specified by the **From Current Frame** setting. A third choice is to choose an image file to represent the video; any of the image types supported by InDesign can be used.

## The Buttons and Forms Panel

The **Buttons and Forms** panel offers a range of settings for the creation of buttons.

The following table lists the different button options and what they are used for.

| Component | Used To |
| --- | --- |
| **Type** | Specify the type of control, such as button, radio button, check box, list box, etc. |
| **Name** | Specify a name for a button. |
| **Event** | Specify the event that initiates the desired action. |
| **Actions** | Identify the action to be taken when the event occurs. |

| Component | Used To |
|-----------|---------|
| **Appearance** | Specify the visual state for the button. |

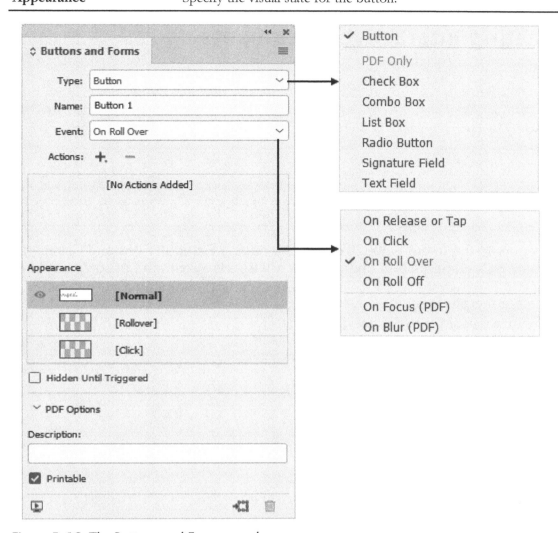

*Figure 5–16: The Buttons and Forms panel.*

**Note:** To learn more about interactivity with InDesign, check out the LearnTO **Create Buttons** presentation from the **LearnTO** tile on the CHOICE Course screen.

Access the Checklist tile on your **CHOICE Course screen for reference information and job aids on How to Create Interactive Documents.**

# ACTIVITY 5–4
## Creating Interactive Documents

### Before You Begin

You previously saved a file as C:\092024Data\Managing External Files and Creating Dynamic Documents\My Sports Brochure Lesson 5b.indd.

### Scenario

The owners of My Footprint Sports are attending a trade show and would like to have you add some interactive elements to the brochure. You decide to add some animation to the cover page.

---

1. Navigate to the folder **C:\092024Data\Managing External Files and Creating Dynamic Documents** and open the file **My Sports Brochure Lesson 5b.indd**.

2. Animate the photo on the cover page.
   a) Navigate to page **1** of the brochure.
   b) With the **Selection** tool, select the photo of the runners.
   c) From the menu, select **Window→Interactive→Animation**.

d) In the **Animation** panel, from the **Preset** drop-down menu, select **Fly in from Left**. The butterfly illustrates the **Fly in from Left** option.

e) In the **Event(s)** section, verify that the **On Page Load** trigger event is selected.
f) From the **Speed** drop-down menu, select **Ease Out**.
   The **Preset** changes to **Custom (Fly in from Left)**, and the butterfly animation is removed.

3. Animate the headline text on the cover page.
   a) Select the text frame containing the headline text "Get where you're going."

    **Note:** You might have to scroll around or hide panels to see the field.

   b) In the **Animation** panel, from the **Preset** drop-down menu, select **Fly in from Right**.
   c) If necessary, in the **Animation** panel, expand the **Properties** section.
   d) In the **Opacity** drop-down menu, verify that **Fade In** is selected.

4. Animate the logo on the cover page.
   a) Select the logo "my footprint sports."
   b) In the **Animation** panel, from the **Preset** drop-down menu, select **Fade In**.

      c) In the **Duration** field, change the value to *0.5*

      d) If necessary, from the **Animate** drop-down menu, select **From Current Appearance**.

      e) If necessary, from the **Opacity** drop-down menu, select **Fade In**.

5. Preview the animation.

    a) Select the **Preview Spread** button at the bottom of the panel.

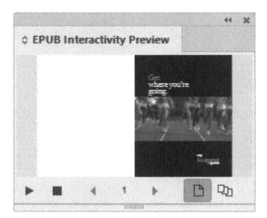

It might take some time for the HTML to be created and the graphic to show up in the EPUB Interactivity Preview window.

    b) To replay the animation, in the **EPUB Interactivity Preview** window, select the **Play** button.

6. Close the **EPUB Interactivity Preview** and the **Animation** panels.

7. Save and close the file.

# Summary

In this lesson, you examined how InDesign allows you to import a layered external file and turn on and off the visibility of the layers to suit your document. You were also able to see how data from an external file, such as a spreadsheet, can be merged into a document. You also organized your document into sections, as well as inserted text variables on document pages and parent pages. Finally, you worked with the interactivity features that can enhance documents exported as PDF documents.

**What are the advantages of working with a layered file?**

**How would you use interactivity features to enhance a document?**

 **Note:** Check your CHOICE Course screen for opportunities to interact with your classmates, peers, and the larger CHOICE online community about the topics covered in this course or other topics you are interested in. From the Course screen you can also access available resources for a more continuous learning experience.

# 6 | Managing Long Documents

**Lesson Time: 1 hour**

## Lesson Introduction

Creating great looking documents is one thing, but building a book requires a whole different set of tools and Adobe® InDesign® has them. There are features for configuring the pagination, assembling the table of contents and the index, as well as footnotes and hyperlinks. In this lesson, you will manage long documents.

## Lesson Objectives

In this lesson, you will:

- Create a book.

- Build a table of contents.

- Create hyperlinks and cross-references.

- Generate an index and insert footnotes.

# TOPIC A

## Create a Book

Assembling a book involves putting together the basic structure for the content. You need to build a table of contents, insert hyperlinks or cross-references, add footnotes, generate an index, and pay attention to pagination and synchronization. In this topic, you will create a book.

### Books

In InDesign, a *book* is a file that consists of a number of individual documents that are merged together. The pages of the documents are sequentially numbered. The table of contents, list of tables, and indices of individual documents are automatically merged when you create a book. The styles and swatches can be synchronized. By default, the first document in the book acts as the style source of the other documents; the style source can be changed as required. You can print either the whole book or selected documents in a book. A book can have up to 1,000 documents and be exported as a PDF document.

 **Note:** Book files have the file extension .indb.

### Pagination

*Pagination* is a method by which content in a document is divided into pages according to a specified page size and margin settings. It defines the appearance of content on a page and the flow of content across pages. Pagination is used to identify the beginning and end of content on pages and for adding page numbers to documents. It is often used to number multi-page documents such as books and web pages.

### The Book Panel

The **Book** panel contains a list of options to create and manipulate a book.

The following lists the various **Book** panel options you can use.

| Option | A button that enables you to: |
|---|---|
| **Synchronize styles and swatches with the Style Source** | Synchronize the styles and swatches of documents with the document set as the style source. |
| **Save the book** | Save a book. |
| **Print the book** | Print either a whole book or only selected documents in a book. |
| **Add documents** | Add documents to a book. |
| **Remove documents** | Remove documents from a book. |

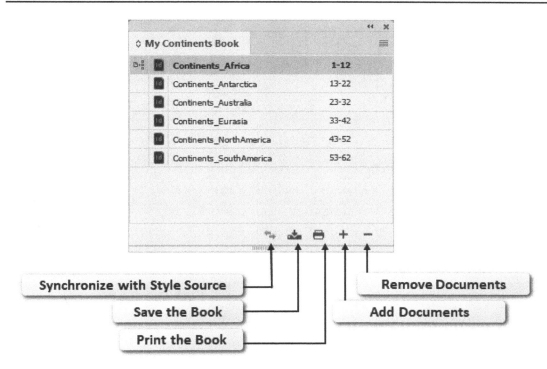

*Figure 6–1: The Book panel.*

# Book Synchronization

When you synchronize documents in a book, the items you specify—styles, variables, parent pages, trap presets, cross-reference formats, conditional text settings, numbered lists, and swatches—are copied from the style source to the specified documents in the book, replacing any items that have identical names. If items in the style source are not found in the documents being synchronized, they are added. Items that are not included in the style source are left as is in the documents being synchronized. You can synchronize the book while documents in the book are closed. InDesign opens the closed documents, makes any changes, and then saves and closes the documents. Documents that are open when you synchronize are changed but not saved.

 **Access the Checklist tile on your CHOICE Course screen for reference information and job aids on How to Create a Book.**

# ACTIVITY 6-1
## Creating a Book

### Data Files

C:\092024Data\Managing Long Documents\Continents_Africa.indd

C:\092024Data\Managing Long Documents\Continents_Antarctica.indd

C:\092024Data\Managing Long Documents\Continents_Australia.indd

C:\092024Data\Managing Long Documents\Continents_Eurasia.indd

C:\092024Data\Managing Long Documents\Continents_NorthAmerica.indd

C:\092024Data\Managing Long Documents\Continents_SouthAmerica.indd

### Scenario

You have been working on a travel book covering all the continents. Each continent was the subject of a document, and now it's time to combine them into the book.

1. Create a book file to add documents.
   a) From the menu, select **File→New→Book**.
   b) In the **New Book** dialog box, navigate to the **C:\092024Data\Managing Long Documents** folder.
   c) In the **File name** text box, type *My Continents Book* and select **Save**.

2. Add documents to the book.

   a) In the **My Continents Book** panel, select the **Add documents** button  and then in the **Add Documents** dialog box, navigate to **C:\092024Data\Managing Long Documents** and select **Continents_Africa.indd, Continents_Antarctica.indd, Continents_Australia.indd, Continents_Eurasia.indd, Continents_NorthAmerica.indd**, and **Continents_SouthAmerica.indd** and select **Open**.

   > **Note:** To quickly select all files, select **Continents_Africa**, press and hold **Shift**, and select **Continents_SouthAmerica**.

b) In the **My Continents Book** panel, verify that the six files appear with their page numbers in sequence.

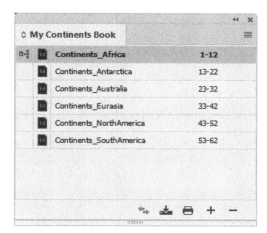

c) Select the **Save the book** button and leave it open.

# TOPIC B

## Build a Table of Contents

Long documents require the inclusion of a table of contents. InDesign aids the designer in this task with this feature. In this topic, you will build a table of contents.

### The Table of Contents

The *table of contents* is an item in a document that helps end users locate information easily. It consists of a list of topics with their page numbers in the order they occur in the document. To create the table of contents, include the paragraph style sheets that determine the text to be included in the table of contents. Character styles can be specified for page numbers and characters between the entry and the number. Entries in the table of contents can be sorted in alphabetical order or according to page numbers. Any number of tables of contents can be created: one for a list of chapters, one for a list of tables, or one for a list of figures used in the document.

## Contents

| | |
|---|---|
| Africa | 3 |
| Antarctica | 13 |
| Australia | 23 |
| Eurasia | 33 |
| North America | 43 |
| South America | 53 |

*Figure 6-2: Table of Contents example.*

### Updates

When you make changes to your document, you will want those changes to be reflected in the table of contents without having to go in and manually update them. You can do this in InDesign because the table of contents is live and can be automatically updated via **Update Table of Contents** in the **Layout** menu.

### The Table of Contents Dialog Box

The **Table of Contents** dialog box contains various options that enable you to format the table of contents.

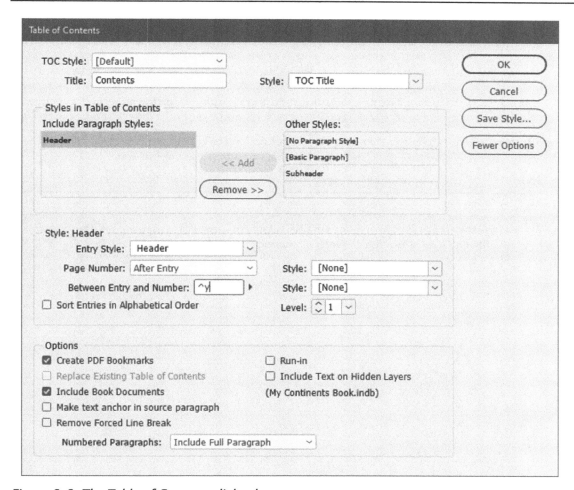

*Figure 6–3: The Table of Contents dialog box.*

The following lists the various options in the **Table of Contents** dialog box and what they do.

| Option | Description |
|---|---|
| **TOC Style** | A drop-down menu that contains the default and custom styles of the table of contents. |
| **Title** | A text box that allows you to specify a name for the TOC style you want to create. |
| **Style** | A drop-down menu that enables you to select a style for the heading. You can also create a style by selecting **New Paragraph Style** from the drop-down menu. |
| **Style in Table of Contents** | A section that allows you to select a paragraph style from the **Other Styles** list box and include the style in the **Include Paragraph Styles** list box. The **Add** and **Remove** buttons enable you to add and remove paragraph styles, respectively, in the table of contents. |
| **Style** | A section that allows you to specify different formatting options for the currently selected styles in the **Include Paragraph Styles** list box using the **Entry Style** drop-down list. When the **More Options** button is selected, additional options that help apply character styles to page numbers and organize the table of contents entries in alphabetical order are displayed. |

| Option | Description |
|---|---|
| **Options** | A section that allows you to create PDF bookmarks, replace existing table of contents, and include a table of contents in the Book document and others when the respective check boxes are checked. You can also specify options using the **Numbered Paragraphs** drop-down menu if the table of contents has paragraph styles with numbers. |
| **More Options** | A button that provides additional options in the **Style** section and allows you to apply styles to the table of contents in various ways. |
| **Save Style** | A button that allows you to save the customized TOC style. |

 **Access the Checklist tile on your CHOICE Course screen for reference information and job aids on How to Build a Table of Contents.**

# ACTIVITY 6-2
## Building a Table of Contents

### Before You Begin
My Continents Book.indd is open.

### Scenario
People who are helping you proofread your Continents book have mentioned that it's hard to navigate quickly to the different sections. You realize that the book needs a table of contents.

---

1. **Specify a paragraph style for the table of contents.**

    a) In the **My Continents Book** panel, double-click the **Continents_Africa** document to open it and navigate to page **1**.

    b) From the menu, select **Layout→Table of Contents**.

    c) In the **Table of Contents** dialog box, from the **Style** drop-down list, select **TOC Title**.

    d) In the **Styles In Table of Contents** section, in the **Other Styles** list box, double-click **Header**.

    e) In the **Style** section, from the **Entry Style** drop-down list, select **Header**.

    f) Select the **More Options** button.

    g) From the **Page Number** drop-down menu, verify that **After Entry** is displayed.

    h) In the **Between Entry and Number** field, double-click to select the current value, select the right arrow button next to it, and from the menu, select **Right Indent Tab**.

    i) If necessary, in the **Options** section, check the **Include Book Documents** check box.

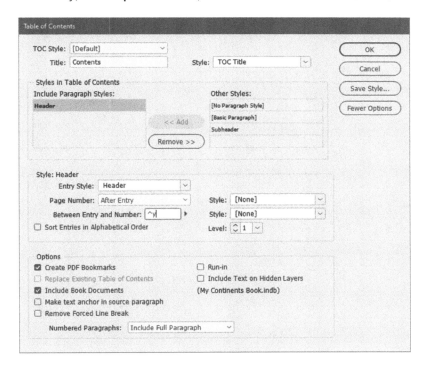

    j) Select **OK**. The cursor becomes a loaded text icon with a preview of the table of contents attached to it.

    k) If you receive a **Warning** dialog box, select **OK**.

---

2. Insert the table of contents into the first page of the first document.

    a) On page **1**, in the top-left corner of the left column, click with the **Loaded Text** icon to insert the table of contents.

    b) On page **1**, verify that the table of contents is displayed.

| Contents | |
|---|---:|
| Africa | 3 |
| Antarctica | 13 |
| Australia | 23 |
| Eurasia | 33 |
| North America | 43 |
| South America | 53 |

    c) Click outside the frame margins to deselect the frame.

    d) Save the **Continents_Africa** file.

3. Save **My Continents Book** and leave it open.

# TOPIC C

## Create Hyperlinks and Cross-References

Designers are now able to take advantage of technology in their documents by inserting interactive features such as cross-references within the document and hyperlinks to external content. In this topic, you will create hyperlinks and cross-references.

## Hyperlinks

A *hyperlink* enables users to navigate to another location. When creating a hyperlink, the source and destination of the hyperlink needs to be specified. The source can be text, text frames, or graphic frames. The destination can be a page or a text anchor in the same document, a different document, or a web page. Hyperlinks can be formatted differently from the rest of the content of a document.

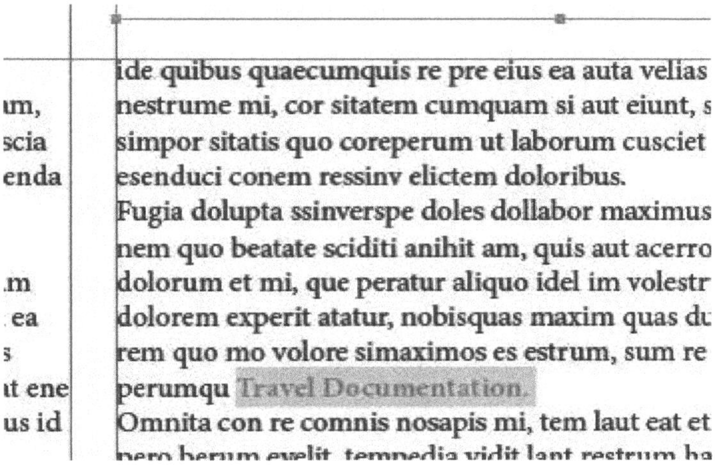

*Figure 6-4: Hyperlinks example.*

## The Hyperlinks Panel

The **Hyperlinks** panel enables you to create and edit hyperlinks. The **Create new hyperlink** button is used to create a hyperlink. You can select the icon at the right to go to the destination to which the text is hyperlinked. The folder icon indicates that the destination is a file instead of a URL. These options are also found on the **Hyperlinks** panel options menu, in addition to options for setting a new destination for a hyperlink, sorting the list of hyperlinks, and setting the hyperlink options.

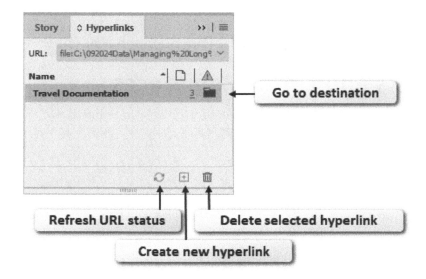

Figure 6–5: The Hyperlinks panel.

## Cross–References

When creating an index, if two or more terms have the same meaning, you can create cross-references for those terms to avoid repetition. There are different types of cross-references.

| Type | Used To |
| --- | --- |
| **See [also]** | Automatically assign correct prefixes to cross-references each time an index is generated. |
| **See** | Cross-reference a topic without page references. |
| **See also** | Cross-reference a topic with page numbers or sub-entries. |
| **See herein** | Refer to a different sub-level entry for details about the current entry. |
| **See also herein** | Refer to a sub-level entry for additional details about the current entry. |

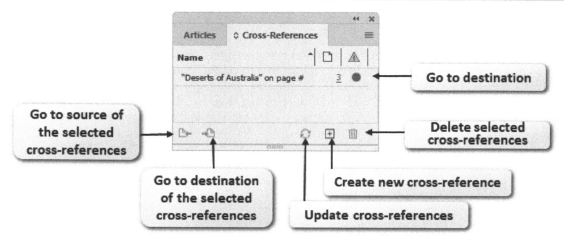

Figure 6–6: The Cross–References panel.

 Access the Checklist tile on your CHOICE Course screen for reference information and job aids on How to Create Hyperlinks and Cross-References.

# ACTIVITY 6–3
## Creating Hyperlinks and Cross-References

### Data Files

C:\092024Data\Managing Long Documents\Travel Documentation.indd

C:\092024Data\Managing Long Documents\My Continents Book.indd

### Before You Begin

My Continents Book.indd is open.

### Scenario

The book could benefit from a link to a related document on travel. You also see the need to add cross-references to other parts of the book.

---

1. Create a hyperlink to another InDesign document.

   a) In **Continents_Africa.indd**, navigate to page **3**.

   b) In the right column, with the **Type** tool, select the text "Travel Documentation."

   c) From the menu, select **Window→Interactive→Hyperlinks** to display the **Hyperlinks** panel.

   d) In the **Hyperlinks** panel, select the **Create new hyperlink** button. ⊞

   e) In the **New Hyperlink** dialog box, from the **Link To** drop-down list, select **File**.

   f) In the **Destination** section, in the **Path** box, select the folder icon and browse to the file **C: \092024Data\Managing Long Documents\Travel Documentation.indd**.

   g) Select **Open**.

   h) In the **Character Style** section, from the **Style** drop-down list, select **[Same style]** and then select **OK**.

   i) Verify that **Travel Documentation** is now listed in the **Hyperlinks** panel.

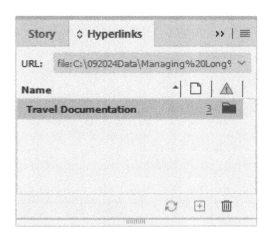

2. Create a cross-reference to another page in the book.

a) Near the bottom of the right column, with the **Type** tool, place the insertion point after the text "desert" and press the **Spacebar**.

maximolor aut mod modisqua
doles etur, iduciis aut deleseq
et poreper chitio. Pudam se co
tur, illorerchil ipit omnis nis m
lab incil imusdae desert |
Omnimagnis quata doluptat e

b) From the menu, select **Window→Type & Tables→Cross-References**. In the **Cross-References** panel, select the **Create new cross-reference** button. ⊞

c) In the **New Cross-Reference** dialog box, in the **Link To** drop-down list, verify that **Paragraph** is selected.

d) In the **Destination** section, from the **Document** drop-down list, select **Browse** and select the file **C:\092024Data\Managing Long Documents\Continents_Australia.indd.** Select **Open**.

e) In the list box, select **Subheader** and verify that **Deserts of Australia** appears in the right pane.

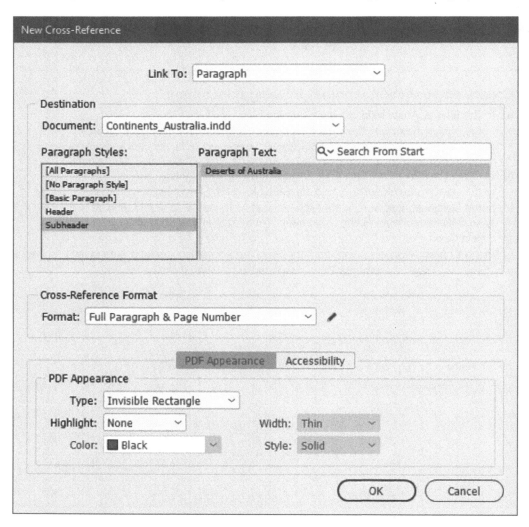

f) Select **OK**.

g) In the **Cross-References** panel, verify that '"Deserts of Australia" on page #' appears. Close the **Cross-References** panel.

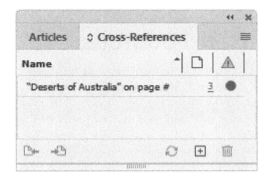

h) In **Continents_Africa.indd**, on page **3**, after the text "desert," verify the text '"Deserts of Australia" on page 25' appears.

> doles etur, iduciis aut deleseq uassitatiae voluptae sit re magnat mo
> et poreper chitio. Pudam se corit quis et fugit laccae. Et aliquis eum
> tur, illorerchil ipit omnis nis moluptatum, simperro cuptaeperro to
> lab incil imusdae desert "Deserts of Australia" on page 25.
> Omnimagnis quata doluptat eium di arum dolorerumqui quati co-

3. Save the **Continents_Africa.indd** file and leave it open.

4. If necessary, save the **My Continents Book**.

# TOPIC D

## Generate an Index and Insert Footnotes

Another feature of long documents and books is an index. The index feature of InDesign offers settings that let you determine how it will be created, what to include, and how it should look. Documenting references in footnotes is essential in composing a long document. The Footnotes feature provides options for collecting and displaying this information in your book. In this topic, you will generate an index and insert footnotes.

### Indexes

An *index* contains a list of words and the page numbers on which these words appear in a document. You can create and organize an index using the **Index** panel. The words in the index are referred to as topics and the page numbers are referred to as page references. Index entries appear as markers that can be made visible and edited. You can edit an index entry by changing the topic name, creating subtopics, and specifying the range of pages when the topic appears on different pages.

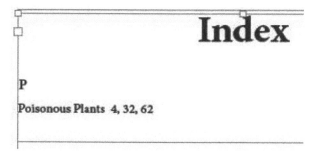

*Figure 6–7: Index example.*

### The Generate Index Dialog Box

The **Generate Index** dialog box has various components that allow you to specify a title, as well as paragraph and character styles for the index items. It also allows you to format the created index.

The following lists what you can configure when generating an index.

| Component | Description |
|---|---|
| **Title** | A text box that allows you to enter a heading for the index. |
| **Title Style** | A drop-down menu that allows you to select a style for the heading. |
| **Replace Existing Index** | A check box that allows you to update an existing index. |
| **Include Book Documents** | A check box that allows you to create a single index for all documents in the current book list and renumber the pages of the book. |
| **Include Entries on Hidden Layers** | A check box that allows you to include index markers for the entries in a document that appear on hidden layers. |
| **More Options** | A button that displays additional index options under sections such as **Level Style**, **Index Style**, and **Entry Separators**. |

| Component | Description |
|---|---|
| **Index formatting options** | A drop-down list that has options such as **Nested** and **Run-in**. The **Nested** option allows you to format the index in the default style where sub-entries are nested under an entry as separate indented paragraphs. The **Run-in** option lets you format all levels of an entry in a paragraph. |
| **Include Index Section Headings** | A check box that allows you to include section headings that have letters of the alphabet. |
| **Include Empty Index Sections** | A check box that allows you to include section headings for all letters of the alphabet, even when the index does not have any first level entries. |
| **Level Style** | A section that allows you to specify styles for different levels of index entries. |
| **Index Style** | A section that allows you to specify a style for the section heading, page number, cross-reference, and cross-referenced topic. |
| **Entry Separators** | A section that allows you to specify the separators to be used between entries and between items in each entry. |

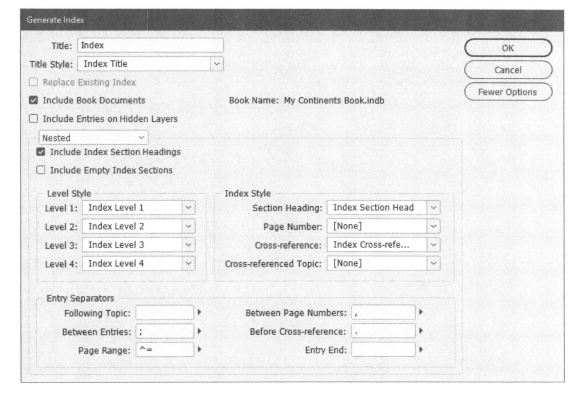

*Figure 6–8: The Generate Index dialog box.*

## Footnotes

A *footnote* is a note placed at the bottom of a page. It is associated with a specific piece of text on the page. It provides additional information about the text or cites references to the source of the text. The reference mark appears beside the text and the footnote; it indicates the association between them.

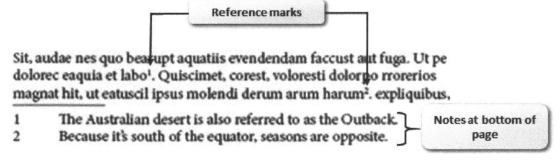

*Figure 6-9: An example of footnote reference markers with footnotes placed at the bottom of a page.*

### Footnotes

Footnotes can span multiple text columns. This can be within a specific frame or across the entire document.

## The Footnote Options Dialog Box

The **Footnote Options** dialog box allows you to format and modify footnotes. The **Numbering and Formatting** tab in the dialog box contains options that enable you to specify the numbering style of footnotes within a document. This tab enables you to format the footnote reference number using one of the available character styles. You can choose a paragraph style to format the footnote text in the document and specify space between the footnote number and start of the footnote text using separators such as **Em space** and **En space**.

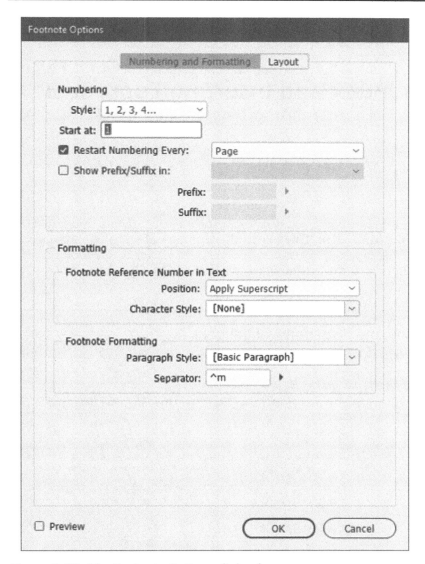

*Figure 6-10: The Footnote Options dialog box.*

 **Access the Checklist tile on your CHOICE Course screen for reference information and job aids on How to Generate an Index and Insert Footnotes.**

## ACTIVITY 6-4
### Generating an Index and Inserting Footnotes

### Before You Begin

My Continents Book, Continents_Africa.indd, and Continents_Australia.indd are open.

### Scenario

In an effort to make locating information easy, you decide that you'll also generate an index that will include terms that encompass the entire book. This will be placed at the end of the last document. And, because there are so many facts being presented in this book, you decide to add footnotes to each page that requires them. Luckily, InDesign makes this possible with the Insert Footnotes feature.

1. Insert index markers into the documents of the book file.

   a) From the menu, select **Window→Type & Tables→Index**, and then in the **Index** panel, check the **Book** check box.

   b) In the **Continents_Africa.indd** file, navigate to page **4**.

   c) Using the **Text** tool, select (highlight) the text "Poisonous Plants" and then from the **Index** panel options menu, select **New Page Reference**.

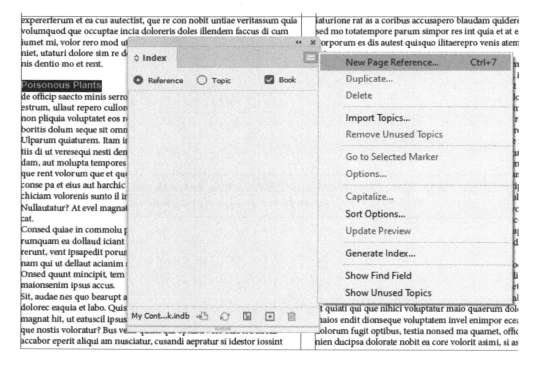

   d) In the **New Page Reference** dialog box, in the **Topic Levels** section, in the first text box, verify that the text **Poisonous Plants** is displayed.

   e) Select **Add**.

   f) Select **Done** to close the **New Page Reference** dialog box.

   g) Switch to the **Continents_Australia.indd** file, navigate to page **32**, select the text "Poisonous Plants," then from the **Index** panel options menu, select **New Page Reference**.

h) In the **New Page Reference** dialog box, in the **Topic Levels** section, in the first text box, verify that the text **Poisonous Plants** is displayed.

i) Select **Add** and then select **Done**.

j) In the **My Continents Book** panel, double-click **Continents_SouthAmerica.indd** and go to page 62.

k) Select the text "Poisonous Plants" and in the **Index** panel, create a new page reference as you did for the same text in **Continents_Africa.indd** and **Continents_Australia.indd**.

l) In the **Index** panel, scroll down and expand the letter **P** and then expand the entry **Poisonous Plants** to display the page numbers that it appears on in the book.

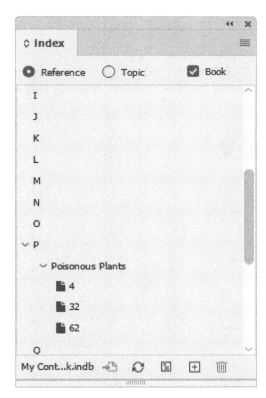

 **Note:** You can check **Book** to display all of the pages that contain a reference to Poisonous Plants.

2. Generate an index and place it in a text frame.

a) In **Continents_SouthAmerica.indd**, open the **Pages** panel.

b) In the **Pages** panel, select the last page (62).

c) Select the **Create New Page** button.

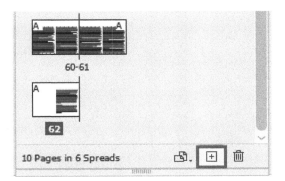

d) Verify that page **63** now appears.

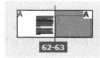

e) In the **Index** panel, select the **Generate Index** button.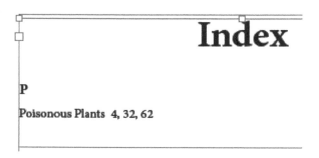
f) In the **Generate Index** dialog box, check the **Include Book Documents** check box, and select **OK**.
g) If you receive a **Warning** dialog box, select **OK**.
h) Verify that the mouse pointer changes to a loaded text icon.
i) On the last page of **Continents_SouthAmerica.indd**, click in the left column to load the index.
j) Verify that the index is placed correctly and that it has one entry under the letter **P** with three page references for that entry.

# Index

**P**

Poisonous Plants  4, 32, 62

3. Add a footnote to the document.

a) In the document **Continents_Australia.indd**, navigate to page 25.
b) In the left column, in the second paragraph, in the first sentence, place the insertion point after the word "Earth" and before the period.
c) From the menu, select **Type→Insert Footnote**.

If the **Footnotes that span columns** box is displayed, select **Close**.

d) Type *Only Antarctica is drier.*

## Deserts of Australia

70% of the Australian mainland is classified as semi-arid, arid or desert; making it the driest inhabited continent on Earth[1].

Bitatusci dolorrovid mod que peribusti to omnis qui sitem aut re voloreh entiscimenis des ent latur, autessim elitatusae nimusae ernam quam, alicidelique deliqui derrunt.Luptatios es utem sunt dolupta dolum que non pe nosam dolendebit, omnis erectatur, odignis erferendi nullab ipsunt. Feriae pro tem. Um nobita ipsum ut as am que dest, ut faccum fugia conem et aut ut omnima dolupta erorior assi vel expero omnis repererum suntia pro verum sam volorestrum faccusdae re pos repe pereptas ratem eum voloratus estio et lat am dus pres ea consequiam, sam conecta num aut fuga. Neque voluptas ut que pe nectium utes qui cus magnis cuptaquiate re, nam volores sinusapere derovid quam, sita enis voluptate voluptat aut exces solorporio cuptur? Del mo essum comnis et alignis

1        Only Antarctica is drier

4. Format the footnote.

   a) From the menu, select **Type→Document Footnote Options**.

   b) In the **Footnote Options** dialog box, on the **Numbering and Formatting** tab, in the **Numbering** section, check the **Restart Numbering Every** check box. From the drop-down list, verify that **Page** is selected.

   c) In the **Footnote Formatting** section, in the **Separator** field, double-click the value to select it.

d) Select the right arrow button and select **Em Space**.

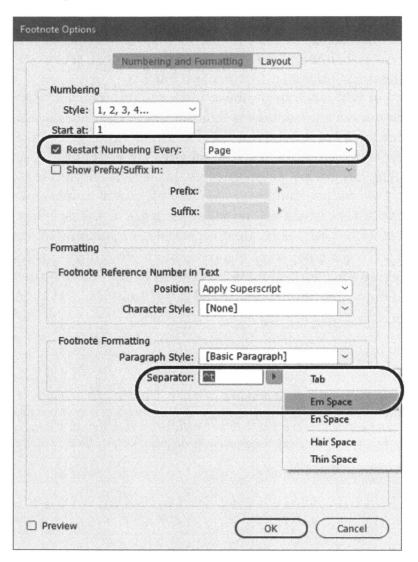

e) Select **OK**.

5. Close the **Index** panel.

6. Save and close all of the .indd files.

7. Save the book and close it.

# Summary

In this lesson, you identified the steps to creating a book. Once the book was developed, you were able to add footnotes, hyperlinks, cross-references, and a table of contents. Finally, you generated an index.

**In what ways might your projects benefit from the Book feature of InDesign?**

**In what ways might you use the Hyperlinks feature?**

 **Note:** Check your CHOICE Course screen for opportunities to interact with your classmates, peers, and the larger CHOICE online community about the topics covered in this course or other topics you are interested in. From the Course screen you can also access available resources for a more continuous learning experience.

# 7 | Publishing InDesign Files for Other Formats and Customizing Print Settings

**Lesson Time: 1 hour, 30 minutes**

## Lesson Introduction

As you develop your document, you must be cognizant of the various ways in which you may need to deliver it. Printers will require that you export it as a PDF file with printer marks and other necessary settings in place. If your document features interactivity, you'll need to know how to export it as an interactive PDF file. You should also consider that your document may need to be made available for e-readers in an EPUB format. As you make final preparations for printing your document, you have a wide range of print settings that you can choose from to customize the printing process to your specifications. You can manage color settings and profiles, preview the print output, and create print presets. In this lesson, you will publish Adobe® InDesign® files for other formats and customize print settings.

## Lesson Objectives

In this lesson, you will:

- Export PDF files for print.

- Export interactive PDF files and files for animation.

- Export files for web.

- Manage colors.

- Preview the print output.

- Create print presets.

# TOPIC A

# Export PDF Files for Print

In preparing to export a document for delivery to a commercial printer, there are a number of settings you'll need to consider, such as printer marks, bleed, compatibility, and compression. In this topic, you will export PDF files for print.

## Grayscale Output

InDesign lets you proof and export designs as grayscale PDFs. Use this feature to quickly export your layout for grayscale printing. The digital publication remains full color, and you can avoid maintaining separate layouts for grayscale and color outputs. Select **View→Proof Setup→Custom** to specify grayscale proof options, and select a **Dot Gain** or **Gamma destination**. After you've set up the proof, select **View→Proof Colors** to toggle between grayscale and color output. You can also export a grayscale PDF from within InDesign. All page items, irrespective of their original color space, are converted to grayscale while exporting to PDF.

## Bleed

The **bleed** area allows you to print objects that are arranged at the outer edge of the defined page size. For a page of the required dimensions, if an object is positioned at its edge, some white may appear at the edge of the printed area due to slight misalignment during printing or trimming. For this reason, you should position an object that is at the edge of the page of the required dimensions a little beyond the edge and trim after printing. The **bleed** area is shown by a red line on the document. You can set bleed area settings in the **Print** dialog box, in the **Marks and Bleed** section.

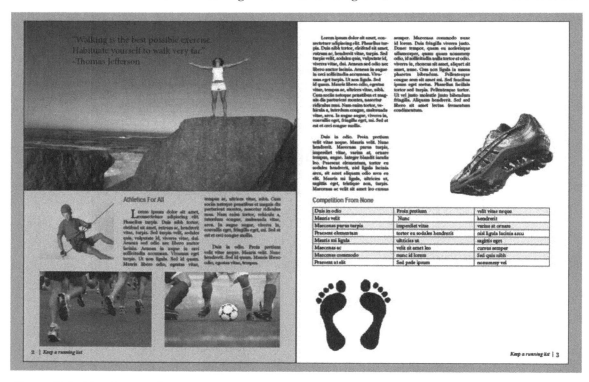

*Figure 7-1: Bleed example.*

# Printer Marks

Printer marks is the term used to describe all the marks on the document that give information to the printer to ensure proper output.

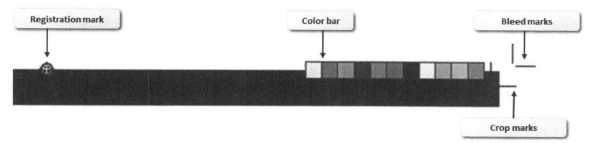

*Figure 7–2: Printer marks.*

The following lists the different types of printer marks.

| Printer Mark | Description |
| --- | --- |
| **Crop marks** | Indicate where the page is trimmed. These marks are thin, vertical or horizontal lines. |
| **Bleed marks** | Ensure that colors are printed up to these marks so the color is at the very edge of a page after trimming. These marks look similar to the crop marks, but appear just outside the latter. |
| **Registration marks** | Ensure that printing plates align with one another. These marks are not required if the image setter punches holes to align a page. |
| **Color bars** | Help the press operator set the density of ink on the press. These appear in gray and colored squares. |
| **Page information** | Contains information such as the file name, page number, date, and time. |

# Compatibility

In order for users with early versions of Adobe® Acrobat® PDF to access your content, you will need to output to the lowest version of PDF available. If you change the version in the **Compatibility** list, the **Adobe PDF Preset** will add the word "modified" to the preset value. For example, if it is set to **[Press Quality]**, it will change to **[Press Quality] [modified]**.

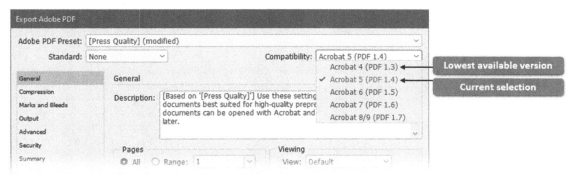

*Figure 7–3: Compatibility choices.*

# Compression

It is best practice to reduce the file size of documents distributed for viewing purposes only. Text, bitmap images, and line art in a document can be compressed to reduce the size of a file exported to PDF. In the **Export Adobe PDF** dialog box, on the **Compression** tab, downsample images to 72 pixels per inch, select automatic compression, and select either low- or medium-image quality for color and grayscale images. When you work with photographic images, use **Automatic (JPEG)** compression; when you work with images that are mostly solid color, such as charts and graphs, use **ZIP** compression.

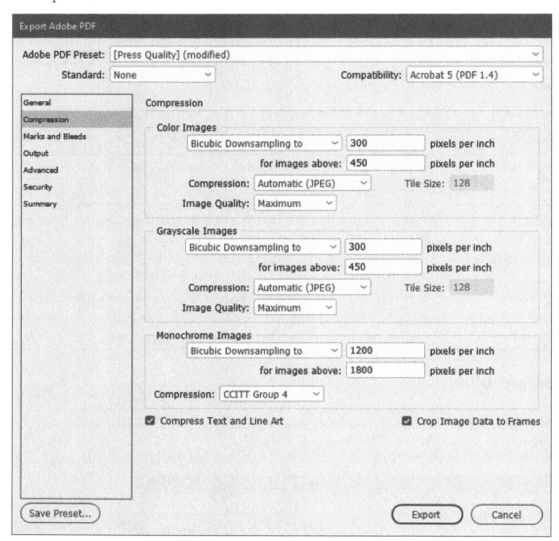

*Figure 7–4: The Compression tab of the Export Adobe PDF dialog box.*

# Output

When exporting to PDF, you can set options on the **Output** tab of the **Export Adobe PDF** dialog box. The interactions between the various output space options will change, depending on a number of factors, including:

- Whether color management is on or off.
- Whether the document has been tagged with color profiles.
- What PDF standard is selected.

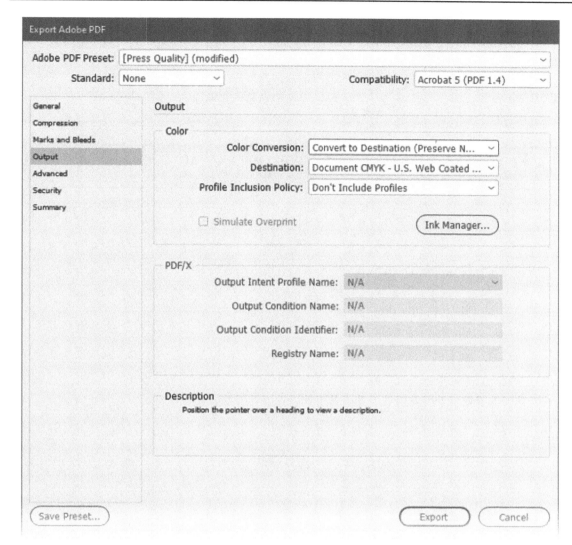

*Figure 7-5: The Output tab of the Export Adobe PDF dialog box.*

| Options | Description |
| --- | --- |
| **Color Conversion** | Allows you to determine how to represent color information. Includes **No Color Conversion**, **Convert to Destination**, and **Convert to Destination (Preserve Numbers)**. |
| **Destination** | Determines the range of the CMYK or RGB output device. |
| **Profile Inclusion Policy** | Allows you to specify whether there is a color profile included in the file. The options are **Include Destination Profile** or **Don't Include Profiles**. |
| **Simulate Overprint** | Allows you to simulate the appearance of printing separations. |
| **Ink Manager** | Allows you to specify ink settings and control whether spot colors will be converted to process equivalents. |
| **Output Intent Profile Name** | Allows you to specify the characterized printing condition for the document. |
| **Output Condition Name** | Determines the print condition you intended. |

| Options | Description |
|---|---|
| **Output Condition Identifier** | Directs you to additional information on the printing condition you intended. |
| **Registry Name** | Shows web addresses pointing to more information on the registry. |

 **Access the Checklist tile on your CHOICE Course screen for reference information and job aids on How to Export PDF Files for Print.**

# ACTIVITY 7–1
## Exporting PDF Files for Print

### Data File

C:\092024Data\Publishing InDesign Files for Other Formats and Customizing Print Settings \Flyer.indd

### Scenario

The flyer you developed for the Scrimdown Playhouse is ready for the printer. In preparation for that, you want to export a PDF file that includes the necessary printer marks.

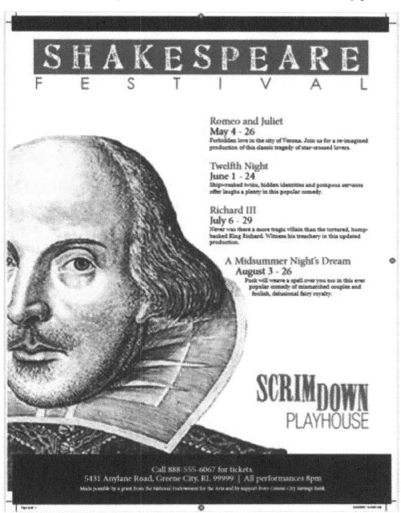

*Figure 7–6: The PDF file with printer marks.*

1. Create a grayscale output to proof the file before exporting to PDF.

    a) Navigate to the folder **C:\092024Data\Publishing InDesign Files for Other Formats and Customizing Print Settings** and open the file **Flyer.indd**.

**Note:** If prompted to update links, select **Update Modified Links.**

b) From the menu, select **File→Export.**

c) In the **Export** dialog box, navigate to the folder **C:\092024Data\Publishing InDesign Files for Other Formats and Customizing Print Settings**, and in the **File name** box, type *Flyer_grayscale*

d) From the **Save as type** drop-down menu, select **Adobe PDF (Print).**

e) Select **Save.**

f) In the **Export Adobe PDF** dialog box, on the **Output** tab, from the **Color Conversion** drop-down list, select **Convert to Destination.**

g) From the **Destination,** drop-down list, select **sGray.** You may need to scroll to view the options at the bottom of the list.

h) On the **General** tab, ensure that **View PDF after Exporting** is checked.

i) Select **Export.**

j) View the PDF and verify that it is grayscale.

k) Close the PDF file.

2. Export the file to PDF with printer marks.

a) From the menu, select **File→Export.**

b) In the **File name** box, type *Flyer with Printer Marks*

c) From the **Save as type** drop-down menu, verify that **Adobe PDF (Print)** is selected.

d) Select **Save.**

e) In the **Export Adobe PDF** dialog box, verify that **View PDF after Exporting** is checked.

f) On the **Marks and Bleeds** tab, in the **Marks** section, check the **Crop Marks, Registration Marks,** and **Page Information** check boxes.

g) In the **Bleed and Slug** section, if necessary, uncheck the **Use Document Bleed Settings** check box.

h) In the **Bleed** section, verify that the **Make all settings the same** button 🔘 is enabled and then change all bleed settings to **.25.**

i) Select **Export.**

j) Verify that the PDF file has crop marks, registration marks, and page information, then close it.

3. Save the file in the **C:\092024Data\Publishing InDesign Files for Other Formats and Customizing Print Settings** folder as *My Flyer.indd* and close the file.

# TOPIC B

# Export Interactive PDF Files

InDesign lets you build PDF files with all the same interactivity that you would if you were using Adobe® Acrobat®. To publish these files, you need to export them as interactive PDF files. In this topic, you will export interactive PDF files and export files for animation.

## The Export to Interactive PDF Dialog Box

When exporting to an interactive PDF file, you have a range of options to consider.

The following describes the export components you can configure.

| Component | Description |
| --- | --- |
| Pages | A radio button that lets you select **All**, **Range**, or specific pages. |
| Create Separate PDF Files | A check box that allows you to create separate PDFs for each page or spread. |
| View | A drop-down list that offers various view settings. |
| Layout | A drop-down list that offers various layout options. |
| Presentation | A check box that offers the ability to **Open in Full Screen Mode**. With that checked, you are then able to specify the rate at which pages flip. |
| Page Transitions | A drop-down list that offers a range of preset page transition animations. |
| Forms and Media | A radio button that allows you to select between **Include All** and **Appearance Only**. |
| Embed Page Thumbnails | A check box that, when selected, embeds a thumbnail preview for each page in the PDF, increasing the file size. It is recommended that you uncheck this setting when users of Acrobat 5.0 and later view and print the PDF, as these versions generate thumbnails dynamically each time you click the **Pages** panel of a PDF. |
| Create Acrobat Layers | A check box that saves each InDesign layer as an Acrobat layer within the PDF. |
| Create Tagged PDF | A check box that gives the option to **Create Tagged PDF**. With that checked, you are then able to check the **Use Structure for Tab Order** check box. |
| Use Structure for Tab Order | A check box that, when selected, uses the tab order specified using **Object→Interactive→Set Tab Order**. This option is only available for tagged PDFs. |

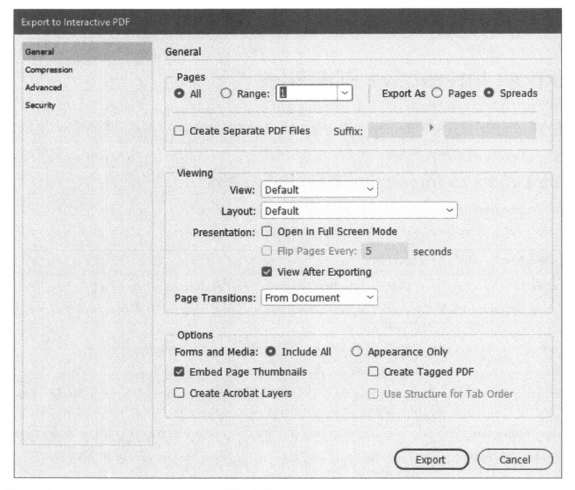

*Figure 7-7: The Export to Interactive PDF dialog box.*

## PDF Form Objects

Sometimes you need to create a PDF form that can be filled out. InDesign supports the creation of PDF form objects without the need to use Adobe Acrobat. You can create and name a form in InDesign and you can add and take away form fields. PDF forms can be created by using the **Buttons and Forms** panel, and any object other than media files can be used as a form.

You can create:

- Button
- Check Box
- Combo Box
- List Box
- Radio Button
- Signature Field
- Text Field

A button can be converted to an object if you need to do so. You can also then change it back to a button, but it will not retain the original button settings you applied.

*Figure 7-8: PDF Buttons and Forms panel.*

 **Access the Checklist tile on your CHOICE Course screen for reference information and job aids on How to Export Interactive PDF Files.**

# ACTIVITY 7-2
## Exporting Interactive PDF Files

### Data Files

C:\092024Data\Publishing InDesign Files for Other Formats and Customizing Print Settings\Sports Brochure Lesson 7.indd

C:\092024Data\Publishing InDesign Files for Other Formats and Customizing Print Settings\Sports Coupon.pdf

### Scenario

Since you're already exporting this as an animated PDF, you decide to add some of the other interactive features that Adobe offers such as bookmarks and buttons. The owners of My Footprint Sports would also like you to save the animation separately for use elsewhere.

1. Create a button to open a coupon.

   a) Navigate to the folder **C:\092024Data\Publishing InDesign Files for Other Formats and Customizing Print Settings** and open the file **Sports Brochure Lesson 7.indd.**

    **Note:** If prompted to update links, select **Update Modified Links.**

   b) On page **3**, using the **Selection** tool, select the orange button with the text "Click for Coupon."

   c) From the menu, select **Window→Interactive→Buttons and Forms.**

   d) From the **Type** drop-down menu, select **Button.**

   e) In the **Name** box, type *Coupon Button*

   f) In the **Actions** section, select the **Add new action for selected event** button ➕ and select **Open File.**

   g) In the **Select File** box, browse to the folder **C:\092024Data\Publishing InDesign Files for Other Formats and Customizing Print Settings** and double-click the **Sports Coupon.pdf** file.

h) In the **PDF Options** section, in the **Description** box, type *Coupon Button*

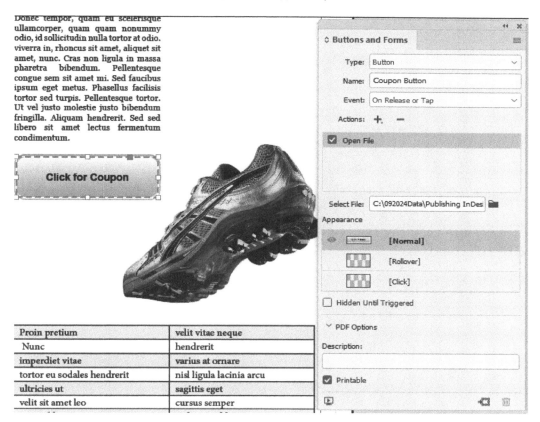

## 2. Add bookmarks to the file.

a) In the **Pages** panel, double-click page **1**.

b) In the **Bookmarks** panel, select the **Create new bookmark** button. Change the default title to *pg1*

c) Repeat steps a and b for all the pages in the document, naming them appropriately, until there are eight bookmarks.

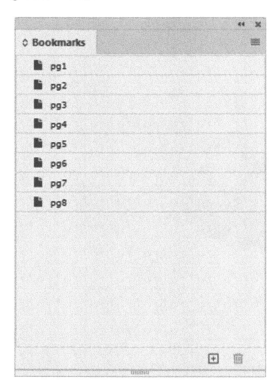

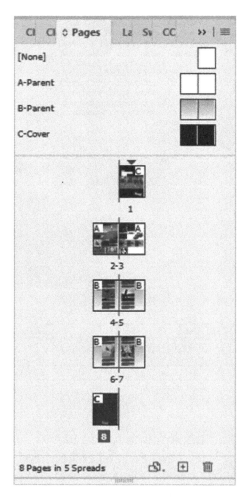

3. Export the file as an interactive PDF file.

a) From the menu, select **File→Export**. Navigate to the folder **C:\092024Data\Publishing InDesign Files for Other Formats and Customizing Print Settings**, and in the **File name** box, type *Interactive Sports Brochure*

b) From the **Save as type** drop-down menu, select **Adobe PDF (Interactive)** and select **Save**.

c) In the **Export to Interactive PDF** dialog box, select **Export**.

 **Note:** If a warning box about switching to **RGB** from **CMYK** appears, select **OK**.

d) Test the bookmarks

e) Select the coupon on page 3, and select **Allow** when prompted to verify that the coupon button works.

 **Note:** In order to select **Allow**, you might need to use the arrow key to highlight it before clicking on it. Otherwise, the PDF reader might close without opening the **Sports Coupon.pdf** file.

f) Close the **PDF** file.

g) Close the **Buttons and Forms** panel and the **Bookmarks** panel.

4. Save the file in the C:\092024Data\Publishing InDesign Files for Other Formats and Customizing Print Settings folder as *My Sports Brochure Lesson 7.indd* and leave it open.

# TOPIC C

## Export Files for the Web

The creation of documents for publishing to the Internet or for use on e-readers requires that you export your document with specific settings for use on the web. In this topic, you will export files for the web.

### Articles

Articles provide an easy way to create relationships among page items. These relationships are used to define the content to export to EPUB, HTML, or Accessible PDFs; and to define the order of the content. You can create articles from a combination of existing page items within a layout, including images, graphics, or text. Once an article has been created, page items can be added, removed, or reordered. Articles can be created manually by dragging one or more page items to an article in the **Articles** panel.

### The Articles Panel

You can manage articles using the **Articles** panel. You can drag page elements into the **Articles** panel to add them to an article. Drag items in the **Articles** panel to change the order or move them from one article to another. The **Articles** panel options menu provides other options to manage content.

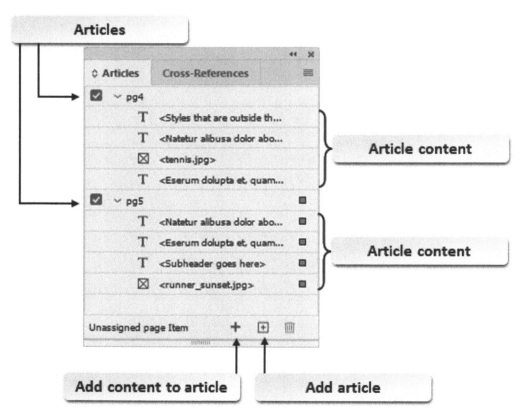

*Figure 7-9: The Articles panel.*

# XHTML

*XHTML*, or eXtensible Hypertext Markup Language, is a markup language that is used to display a document in a browser such as Internet Explorer. It is case-sensitive and its tags are in lowercase. XHTML markup is extensible because it can also be created by the end user.

## HTML Export Options

You can export the entire document or select components from the document. In addition, you can change the order of the content. Style sheet specifications can be manged on the **Advanced** tab of the **HTML Export Options** dialog box. Depending on whether the quality of the images is more important or the speed at which the viewer can see the images, you can change image options on the **Image** tab.

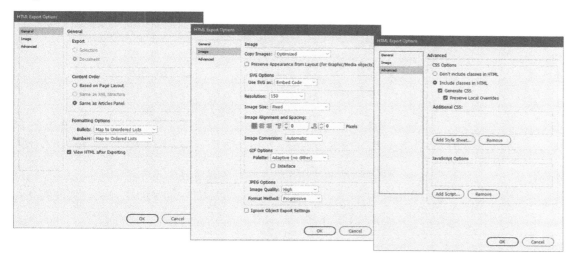

*Figure 7–10: Configure the HTML options.*

# EPUB

You can export a document or book as a reflowable eBook in EPUB format that is compatible with the Adobe® Digital Editions reader software, and other eBook reader software. InDesign creates a single .epub file containing the XHTML-based content. If specified, the exported file may include a cover image. The cover image is created from an image, or created from a JPEG thumbnail image from the first page in the specified document (or the style source document if a book was selected). The thumbnail is used to depict the book in the EPUB readers or the Digital Editions Reader library view. To view the file, you need an EPUB reader, such as Adobe Digital Editions.

You can export in fixed layout or reflowable layout. Reflowable is useful if you will be giving readers options to change the size of text in their e-reader device. Documents containing large amounts of graphics, or video or audio content are best exported using the fixed layout. If your document includes hyperlinks, page transitions, navigation buttons, and animations, it is suggested that you use fixed layout.

## The EPUB Reflowable Layout Export Options Dialog Box

The **EPUB Reflowable Layout Export Options** dialog box contains eight tabs offering a range of options.

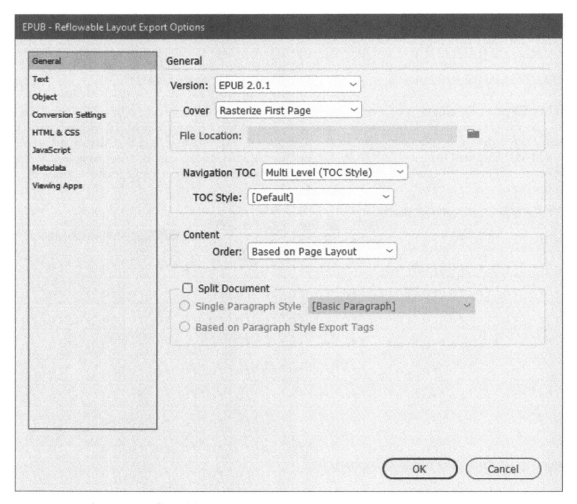

*Figure 7-11: The EPUB Reflowable Layout Export Options dialog box.*

The following lists the settings you can configure when exporting to EPUB format.

| Tab | Description |
| --- | --- |
| **General** | A tab that offers general EPUB settings. These include **Version**, **Cover**, **Navigation TOC**, and **Content Order**. |
| **Text** | A tab that offers text-related EPUB settings for removing forced line breaks, footnote placement, and mapping of bulleted and numbered lists. |
| **Object** | A tab that offers EPUB image settings. These include **Preserve Appearance from Layout**; **Object Size, Layout, and Spacing**; **Insert Page Break**; and **Ignore Object Export Settings**. |
| **Conversion Settings** | A tab that offers specifications for handling conversions. These include **Resolution, JPEG Options, GIF Options**, and **PNG Options**. |
| **HTML & CSS** | A tab that offers EPUB settings for generating HTML and CSS, including **Margins**. **Preserving Local Overrides**, and **Including Embeddable Fonts**. |
| **Javascript** | A tab that contains the list of Javascript files included in this EPUB document. |
| **Metadata** | A tab that contains the Metadata information, such as the **Identifier**, **Title**, and the name of the **Creator**. |

| Tab | Description |
| --- | --- |
| **Viewing Apps** | A tab that specifies the application used to view the EPUB after export. The system default is Adobe Digital Editions. |

 **Access the Checklist tile on your CHOICE Course screen for reference information and job aids on How to Export Files for the Web.**

# ACTIVITY 7-3
## Exporting Files for the Web

### Before You Begin

My Sports Brochure Lesson 7.indd is open.

Adobe Digital Editions is installed on your computer.

### Scenario

In order to keep up with the many ways content is being delivered these days, the owners of My Footprint Sports want you to investigate how easy it would be to convert some of the brochure for tablets and eReaders.

1. Create an article from the items on page 4.

   a) Navigate to page **4** and select all the text and images on the page. If necessary, zoom out so you can easily see the entire page 4 spread, and with the **Selection** tool, drag across page 4 to select its contents.

      Make sure you only drag across page 4. Do not include anything from page 5.

   b) From the menu, select **Window→Articles**.

   c) Drag the selected items from page **4** into the **Articles** panel.

   d) In the **New Article** dialog box, in the **Name** box, type *pg4* and verify that the **Include When Exporting** check box is checked.

   e) Select **OK**.

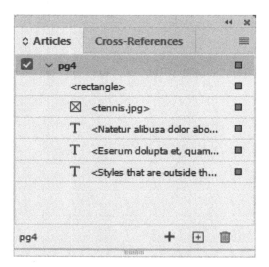

   f) In the **Articles** panel, select **<rectangle>** and select the **Remove** button. 🗑

g) Reorder the items by dragging them so they are in the following order from top to bottom:
  - <Styles that are outside the box...
  - <Natetur alibusa...
  - <tennis.jpg>
  - <Eserum dolupta et,...

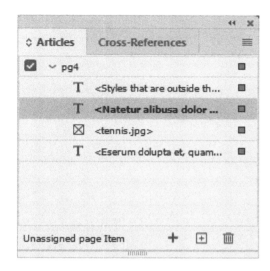

## 2. Export page 4 of the brochure for the web.

a) From the menu, select **File→Export**.

b) In the **Export** dialog box, if necessary, navigate to the **C:\092024Data\Publishing InDesign Files for Other Formats and Customizing Print Settings** folder.

c) In the **File name** box, type *pg4* and from the **Save as type** drop-down menu, select **HTML**.

d) Select **Save**.

e) In the **HTML Export Options** dialog box, in the **Content Order** section, select **Same as Articles Panel**.

f) Verify that the **View HTML after Exporting** check box is checked.

g) On the **Image** tab, in the **Image Alignment and Spacing** section, select the **Align Left** option.

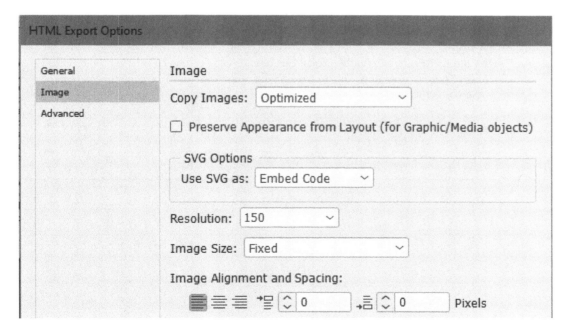

h) Select **OK**. The exported page opens in the browser window.

    i) View page **4** of the brochure in the Internet browser window.

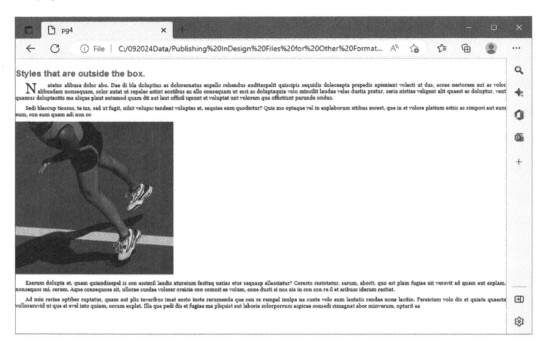

    j) Close the browser window.

3. **Export page 4 of the brochure for EPUB.**
   a) From the menu, select **File→Export**.
   b) In the **Export** dialog box, in the **File name** box, if necessary, type *pg4* and from the **Save as type** drop-down menu, select **EPUB (Reflowable)**.
   c) Select **Save**.
   d) In the **EPUB - Reflowable Layout Export Options** dialog box, on the **General** tab, from the **Content Order** drop-down list, select **Same as Articles Panel**.
   e) Select the **Object** tab, and then in the **CSS** section, from the **Layout** drop-down list, select **Align Left**.
   f) Select the **Viewing Apps** tab and verify that the **System Default** setting for viewing the EPUB document is checked and set to **DigitalEditions.exe**.
   g) Select **OK**.
   h) Review the EPUB page in Adobe Digital Editions.
   i) Close **pg4.epub**. If prompted that the file was not open from the library and asked if you would like to copy it to the library, select **Cancel**.

4. **Close the Articles panel.**

5. **Save and close My Sports Brochure Lesson 7.indd.**

# TOPIC D

# Manage Colors

It's important to review your color settings before handing off the document. Considerations such as color profiles, transparency blend space, and other settings must be reconciled in order to avoid possible delays involving color later on. In this topic you, will manage colors.

## Color Management

*Color management* is the process of matching colors between devices such as a computer monitor and a printer. Color management typically consists of software to profile or characterize each device, and transform the colors in images based on the intended output. Color management may also use hardware to calibrate devices.

## Color Profiles

When you enable color management in the **Assign Profiles** dialog box, you can designate color profiles for RGB and CMYK colors that are applicable to the document. InDesign accepts color management profiles embedded in images and graphics, so the profiles can adjust the color of Adobe® Photoshop® and Adobe® Illustrator® images that were prepared in different color spaces. You can also control how to handle profile mismatches and missing profiles in the **Color Settings** dialog box.

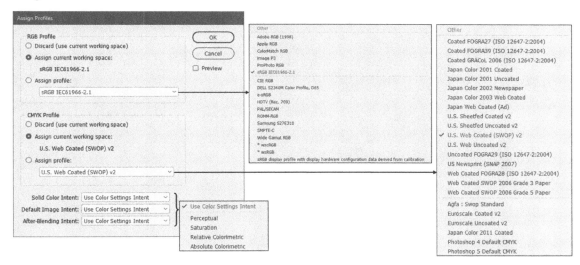

*Figure 7-12: You can manage color profiles in InDesign.*

## Spot Colors and Process Colors

A *spot color* is a color that is printed with only one ink. Spot colors are used to replicate colors accurately and consistently. The combination of inks mixed according to the manufacturer's formula and the paper on which the color is printed determines the exact appearance of the spot color.

A *process color* is a color that is printed with four standard inks on four separate plates. It is a combination of the four offset inks: Cyan, Magenta, Yellow, and Black. These are collectively referred to as CMYK.

## Transparency Blend Space

If you apply transparency to objects on a spread, all colors on that spread convert to the transparency blend space you've chosen (**Edit→Transparency Blend Space**), either **Document RGB** or **Document CMYK**, even if they're not involved with transparency. Converting all the colors results in consistency across any two same-colored objects in a spread and avoids more dramatic color behavior at the edges of transparency. Colors are converted as you draw objects. Colors in placed graphics that interact with transparency are also converted to the blend space. This affects how the colors appear on-screen and in print, but not how the colors are defined in the document.

## The Color Settings Dialog Box

You can set up color management using the **Color Settings** dialog box. The **Settings** drop-down menu provides various preset color settings that are best suited for color management in varied workflows. When you select a preset color setting, InDesign automatically applies default settings to the **Working Spaces** and **Color Management Policies** sections. You can also customize the preset color settings by selecting the **Custom** option.

In the **Color Settings** dialog box, the **Working Spaces** section provides an intermediate color space that is used to define and edit colors in Adobe applications. You can also set color management policies that specify how the application handles data when an image is opened or imported using this dialog box. The **Description** section displays information about the color settings.

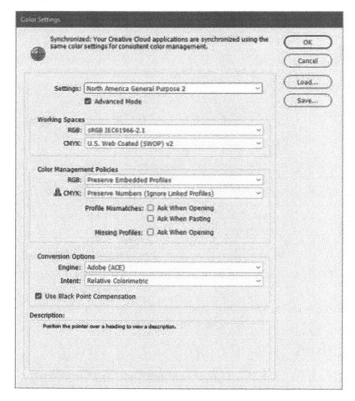

*Figure 7-13: The Color Settings dialog box.*

## Mixed RGB and CMYK Workflows

Creative professionals can mix RGB and CMYK content—and their advantages—in a single, safe, and accurate workflow using InDesign. Its features let print professionals use their current CMYK workflow and keep CMYK graphics protected, as they add RGB content—increasingly available from digital cameras to high-quality stock image libraries and more easily repurposed.

A mixed RGB-CMYK color workflow requires a safe approach to avoid unexpected color conversions and preserve blacks without introducing other colors. Both Illustrator and InDesign employ a safe CMYK mode to preserve CMYK color numbers all the way to the final output. In particular, the safe CMYK mode preserves blacks and ensures that they are not accidentally re-separated.

 **Access the Checklist tile on your CHOICE Course screen for reference information and job aids on How to Manage Colors.**

# ACTIVITY 7–4
## Managing Colors

### Data File

C:\092024Data\Publishing InDesign Files for Other Formats and Customizing Print Settings \Playbill.indd

### Scenario

In order to get the best color output from your printer, you decide to assign the most appropriate color profile considering the paper stock it will be printed on.

---

1. Navigate to the folder **C:\092024Data\Publishing InDesign Files for Other Formats and Customizing Print Settings** and open the file **Playbill.indd**.

    **Note:** If prompted to update links, select **Update Modified Links**.

2. Navigate to page **1** of the file.

3. From the menu, select **Edit→Assign Profiles**.

4. In the **Assign Profiles** dialog box, in the **CMYK Profile** section, select **Assign profile**, and from the drop-down list, select **U.S. Sheetfed Coated v2**.

5. Check the **Preview** check box. Verify that the colors darkened. The change might be quite subtle.

6. Select **OK**.

7. Save the file in the **C:\092024Data\Publishing InDesign Files for Other Formats and Customizing Print Settings** folder as *My Playbill.indd* and leave it open.

---

# TOPIC E

## Preview the Print Output

It is always considered a best practice to review a test print before you hand off to a commercial printer. InDesign features a number of settings so you can get the best idea of how your document will look after being printed. In this topic, you will preview the print output.

### Overprint

*Overprint* is a print technique that makes the top-most color of overlapping shapes transparent. This technique is used to avoid gaps between colors and is supported only by separation devices. While printing, the colors in the overlapping area are blended to form a new color. The **Attributes** panel is used to set up overprinting, and the *Overprint preview* command on the **View** menu is used to preview the overprints. Created overprints can be simulated or discarded using the **Print** dialog box.

### Separations

When artwork is given for printing, the printer separates the artwork into four plates—Cyan, Magenta, Yellow, and Black. These four colors combine to print the actual image. The four plates are created using films which are called separations. The process of separating artwork into different colors is called *color separation*.

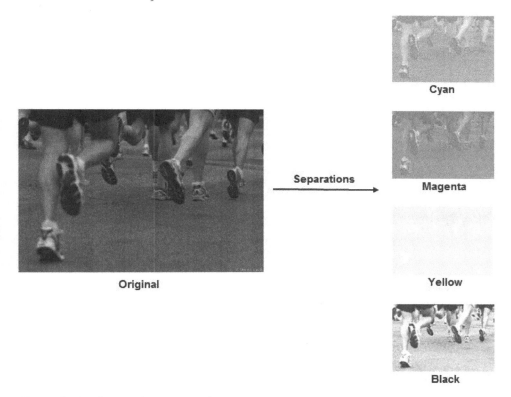

*Figure 7–14: Separations example.*

# The Separations Preview Panel

The **Separations Preview** panel enables you to preview the color separation of a file before printing it. This would help you to troubleshoot common printing issues that may occur in commercial printing. You can use the **Ink Limit** option to identify whether the ink limit has exceeded the specified limit and then control the density of the ink, using the options provided in the **Ink Manager**. You can also use the **Ink Manager** to convert spot colors to process inks, so that the image is reproduced accurately. In addition, the **Ink Manager** allows you to specify the desired color and use standard lab values for reproducing spot colors.

  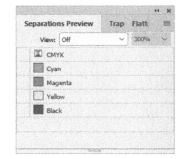

*Figure 7–15: The Separations Preview panel with three different View options.*

# Flattening

*Flattening* is the process that isolates areas where transparent objects overlap other objects. It divides the artwork into components and determines if it can be represented using vector data or if it needs to be rasterized.

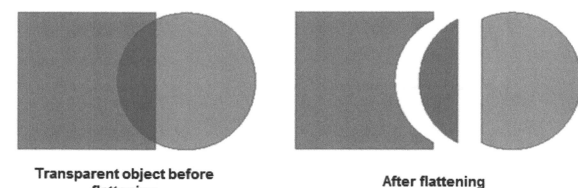

**Transparent object before flattening**

**After flattening**

*Figure 7–16: An example of a transparency after flattening.*

# The Flattener Preview Panel

The **Flattener Preview** panel enables you to preview the areas that will be affected by flattening. The options in the **Highlight** drop-down menu enable you to specify the areas to be highlighted. This panel also contains options for refreshing the highlights and selecting a flattener preset for the document. The **Flattener Preview** panel options menu enables you to create, edit, and load flattener presets.

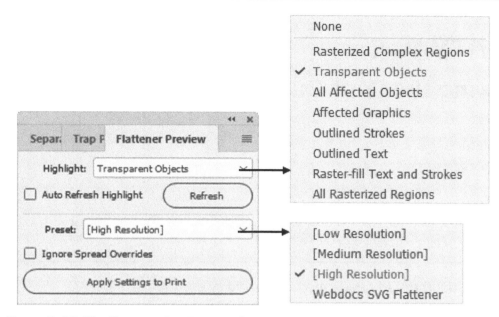

*Figure 7-17: The Flattener Preview panel.*

## Booklet Spreads

The **Print Booklet** feature (**File→Print Booklet**) lets you create printer spreads for professional printing. For example, if you're editing an 8-page booklet, the pages appear in sequential order in the layout window. However, in printer spreads, page 2 is positioned next to page 7, so that when the two pages are printed on the same sheet, folded, and collated, the pages end up in the appropriate order. The process of creating printer spreads from layout spreads is called imposition. While imposing pages, you can change settings to adjust spacing between pages, margins, bleed, and creep. The layout of your InDesign document is not affected, because the imposition is all handled in the print stream. No pages are shuffled or rotated in the document.

 **Access the Checklist tile on your CHOICE Course screen for reference information and job aids on How to Preview the Print Output.**

# ACTIVITY 7-5
## Previewing the Print Output

### Before You Begin

My Playbill.indd is open.

### Scenario

In order to avoid any unpleasant, costly surprises, you decide to preview the print output such as overprint, separations, and flattener within InDesign before you send it out to the printer.

---

1. **Preview the document to check the colors and overprint.**
   a) From the menu, select **View→Overprint Preview**. **Overprint Preview** should now have a check mark to show it's enabled.
   b) From the menu, select **View→Proof Colors** to enable it.
   c) Scroll through the document ending on page 3 to verify the quality of the colors.

2. **Preview separations.**
   a) From the menu, select **Window→Output→Separations Preview**.
   b) In the **Separations Preview** panel, from the **View** drop-down list, verify that **Separations** is selected.

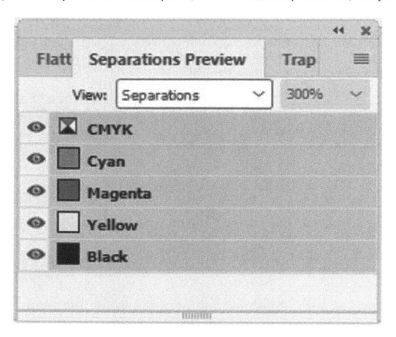

   c) Select the toggle visibility **Eye icon**  of **Cyan** and **Magenta** to view the amount of **Yellow** that will print on each page.

   > **Note:** If the photograph on page 3 is visible, you will see the immediate results of hiding cyan and magenta. When you hover the mouse pointer over the photograph, the percentage for each color is displayed in the **Separations Preview** panel.

d) Restore the visibility of **Cyan** and **Magenta** and close the **Separations Preview** panel.

3. View the transparency of the objects in the document.

a) From the menu, select **Window→Output→Flattener Preview**.

b) In the **Flattener Preview** panel, from the **Highlight** drop-down list, select **Transparent Objects**.

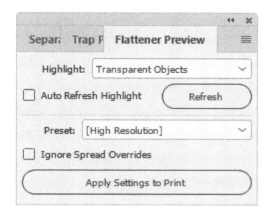

c) On page 2, verify that the rose image is highlighted and appears correctly.

d) Close the **Flattener Preview** panel group.

4. If necessary, save the file. Leave the file open.

# TOPIC F

## Create Print Presets

A time-saving feature you should consider is creating print presets. All your print settings can be saved as a custom preset for future use on similar projects. In this topic, you will create print presets.

### Print Presets

*Print presets* are settings that determine the print output of a file. You can customize the print settings and the type of the printer used to suit your requirements. The saved presets will be available for any document within the application. Print presets can be created either by defining them or by saving the current print settings.

### Trapping

When a document page contains multiple colors, more than one ink color has to be used for printing. The inks used must align properly. When inks do not align, gaps may occur between two different colors. This process of filling the gaps between different colors of overlapping objects is called *trapping*.

### The Ink Manager Dialog Box

The **Ink Manager** dialog box provides control over inks at print output. The output is affected when you make changes to it using the **Ink Manager** and not when colors are defined in the document. For example, when a document includes a spot color, the options of the **Ink Manager** dialog box are used to change the spot color to its equivalent CMYK process color. You can access the **Ink Manager** dialog box from within the **Print** dialog box by selecting the **Output** tab and then selecting **Ink Manager**.

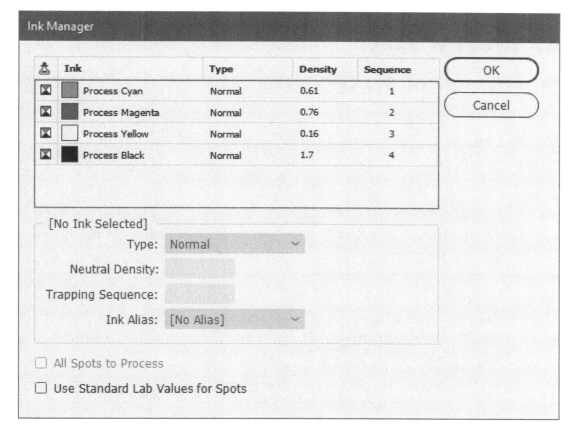

*Figure 7-18: The Ink Manager dialog box.*

## Printer Driver

You may have more than one type of printer in your office and you might print to each of them on different occasions. To change your printer driver settings, in Windows you can use the **Setup** button and in the Mac OS you can use the **Page Setup** or **Printer** button. However, chances are good that your printer driver settings are saved in the **Print** dialog box in InDesign and you can change your printer driver there. Using the **Print** dialog box is the easiest way and you generally only need to go to the **Setup** or **Printer** buttons if there is an option you need that InDesign cannot handle.

 **Access the Checklist tile on your CHOICE Course screen for reference information and job aids on How to Create Print Presets.**

# ACTIVITY 7-6
## Creating Print Presets

### Before You Begin
My Playbill.indd is open.

### Scenario
The Romeo & Juliet playbill is ready for the printer. Since this will be the first of many productions at Scrimdown Playhouse requiring a playbill, it seems smart to create a print preset that will keep the look of the playbills consistent.

1. Select the printer.
   a) Select **File→Print Presets→Define**.
   b) In the **Print Presets** dialog box, select **New**.
   c) In the **New Print Preset** dialog box, in the **Name** box, type *Scrimdown Playbill*
   d) From the **Printer** drop-down list, select **PostScript® File**.
   e) From the **PPD** drop-down list, verify that **Device Independent** is selected.
   f) On the **General** tab, in the **Pages** section, select **Spreads**.

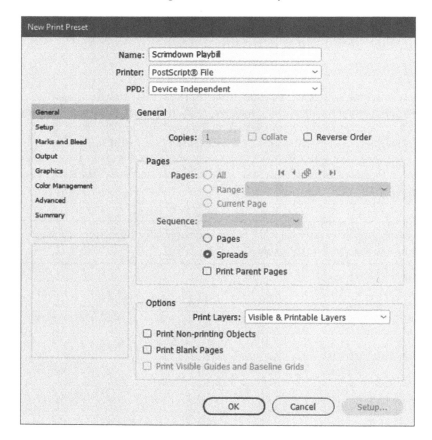

2. Specify the print settings.

a) On the **Marks and Bleed** tab, check the **All Printer's Marks** check box.

b) In the **Bleed and Slug** section, uncheck **Use Document Bleed Settings**.

c) If necessary, verify that the **Make all settings the same** button 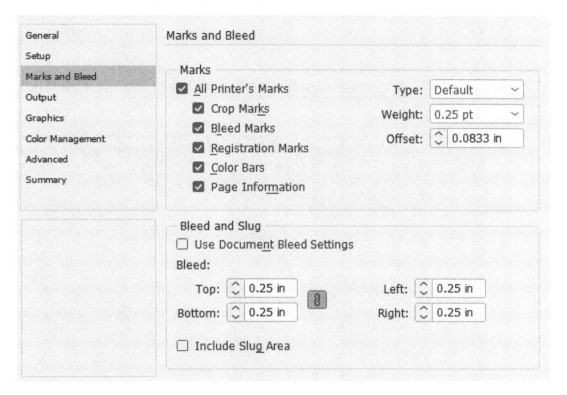 is enabled.

d) Change the setting for **Top** to *.25*

e) If necessary, select the **Make all settings the same** button 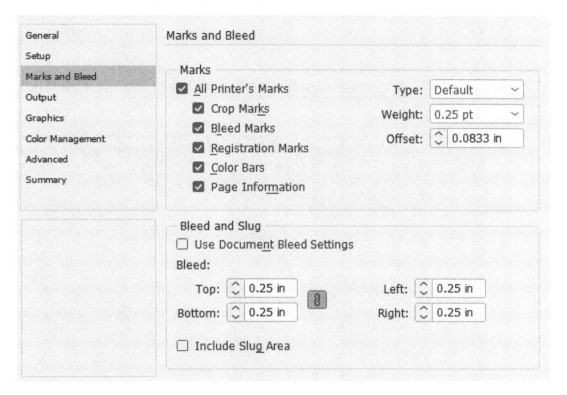 again to enable it. Observe that the **Top**, **Bottom**, **Left**, and **Right** settings all change to *.25*.

f) Select **OK** to save the print settings.

g) In the **Print Presets** dialog box, select **Save**.

h) In the **Save Print Presets** dialog box, in the **File name** text box, type *Scrimdown Playbill* and select **Save**.

i) In the **Print Presets** dialog box, select **OK**.

j) Close the file. If prompted, save the file.

# Summary

In this lesson, you examined the process used to export InDesign documents to other formats such as Adobe PDF for printing, HTML, and EPUB for the web. You also identified how to manage colors, create print presets, and preview print output.

**How does the Articles panel assist in the task of exporting your document for other formats?**



**What are some of the things you need to consider when you are exporting documents to other formats?**

**Note:** Check your CHOICE Course screen for opportunities to interact with your classmates, peers, and the larger CHOICE online community about the topics covered in this course or other topics you are interested in. From the Course screen you can also access available resources for a more continuous learning experience.

# Course Follow–Up

In this course, you developed layouts for multiple formats and took advantage of advanced page elements in Adobe® InDesign®. You applied and managed styles and created complex paths. You also learned about all the options available to make your document interactive and how to work with external files. You managed long documents, published to other formats, and customized print settings.

## What's Next?

Now that you've completed the *Adobe® InDesign® CC: Part 2* course, you may want to add to your design and media knowledge by taking the following Logical Operations course:

*   *Adobe® Photoshop® CC: Part 1*
*   *Adobe® Illustrator® CC: Part 1*

You are encouraged to explore InDesign further by actively participating in any of the social media forums set up by your instructor or training administrator through the **Social Media** tile on the CHOICE Course screen.

# A | Mapping Course Content to the Adobe Certified Professional in Print & Digital Media Publication Using Adobe InDesign Exam

Currently, through **Certiport.com**, Adobe offers the Adobe Certified Professional certification program. Candidates who wish to obtain Adobe Certified Professional in Print & Digital Media Publication Using Adobe InDesign certification must pass the associated exam.

To assist you in your preparation for the exam, Logical Operations has provided a reference document that indicates where the current exam objectives are covered in the Logical Operations *Adobe® InDesign® CC* courseware.

The exam-mapping document is available from the **Course** page on CHOICE. Log on to your CHOICE account, select the tile for this course, select the **Files** tile, and download and unzip the course files. The mapping reference will be in a subfolder named **Mappings**.

Best of luck in your exam preparation!

# B | Productivity Enhancements

## Appendix Introduction

The following are enhancements that were originally introduced in Adobe® InDesign® (2020).

# TOPIC A

## InDesign Productivity Enhancements

Various enhancements in InDesign are offered to increase productivity.

### Split Window

To compare two different layouts in the same document, you can split the active window. Use the two panes to view alternative layouts side by side.

 **Access the Checklist tile on your CHOICE Course screen for reference information and job aids on How to Set the Split Window View.**

 **Access the Checklist tile on your CHOICE Course screen for reference information and job aids on How to Set the Display of Recently Used Fonts.**

 **Access the Checklist tile on your CHOICE Course screen for reference information and job aids on How to Align to Key Object.**

### Save Backward to Earlier Versions

To open an InDesign document in a previous version, or to send it to someone who has not upgraded yet, save the document in the **InDesign Markup Language (IDML)** format. IDML files are supported by InDesign CS4 or later. Features not supported by the earlier version will not work.

 **Access the Checklist tile on your CHOICE Course screen for reference information and job aids on How to Save Backward to Earlier Versions.**

### Export and Proof Grayscale PDFs

You can now proof and export designs as grayscale PDFs. For example, use this feature to quickly export your layout for grayscale printing. The digital publication remains full color, and you can avoid maintaining separate layouts for grayscale and color outputs.

Use **Proof Setup** (**View→Proof Setup→Custom**) to specify grayscale proof options, and select a **Dot Gain**, **Gray Gamma**, or **sGray** destination. After you've setup the proof, select **View→Proof Colors** to toggle between grayscale and color output.

You can also export a grayscale PDF from within InDesign. All page items, regardless of their original color space, are converted to grayscale while exporting to PDF.

Grayscale destinations are not available under the PDF/X-1a standard. The standard supports only CMYK intents. Similarly, PDF/X-2 or PDF/X-3 standards do not support Gamma Gray destinations.

 **Access the Checklist tile on your CHOICE Course screen for reference information and job aids on How to Export Grayscale PDFs.**

# Complex Calculations in Panels and Dialog Boxes

You can now perform complex calculations within the text fields in panels and dialog boxes. Enter a mathematical expression by using mathematical operators; for example, 120p0/2 + 10.

 **Access the Checklist tile on your CHOICE Course screen for reference information and job aids on How to Export to PNG.**

 **Access the Checklist tile on your CHOICE Course screen for reference information and job aids on How to Export Enhancements.**

# C | InDesign Language Support

Adobe® World-Ready Composer and support for open-source Hunspell dictionaries enable you to use several additional languages using InDesign.

## Placeholder Text with Specified Alphabet

You can enter placeholder text in Roman, Arabic, Hebrew, Chinese, among others.

To specify the language of placeholder text, press **Ctrl** when you select **Type→Fill With Placeholder Text**. In the **Fill With** drop-down list, select an alphabet and select **OK**.

## Hunspell Enhancements

For most languages, InDesign ships with open-source Hunspell dictionaries and Hunspell is the default dictionary provider. You can download and install additional spelling and hyphenation dictionaries for other languages from the OpenOffice® website.

To use InDesign with additional languages, select **Edit→Preferences→Dictionary** and adjust the settings as needed.

## Indic Support

Adobe® World-Ready Composer (WRC) provides correct word shaping for many of the non-Western scripts, such as Devanagari. Adobe World-Ready Composers in the International English version of InDesign support several Indian languages, including Hindi, Marathi, Gujarati, Tamil, Punjabi, Bengali, Telugu, Oriya, Malayalam, and Kannada.

Hunspell spelling and hyphenation dictionaries are included, and so is the Adobe Devanagari font family.

Enable the Adobe World-Ready Composer through a paragraph style by opening the **Paragraph** panel and then selecting **Justification**.

Set Indic preferences to work on Indic scripts, and correctly import content into InDesign.

1. Select **Window→Utilities→Scripts**.
2. Expand **Application**, then double-click **Indic Preferences**.
3. Open a new document or restart InDesign.

## Middle Eastern Support

InDesign is also available in Middle Eastern and North African editions. It adds support for Arabic and Hebrew, and provides several features for working with right-to-left, bi-directional scripts, and other language-specific features. Enhanced functionality includes support for tables in the **Story Editor**, improved Kashida justification, enhanced diacritic positioning, and other text-handling improvements.

### South-East Asian Languages

A text engine that supports Thai, Burmese, Lao, Khmer, and Sinhala languages has been added. Documents containing text in those languages can now be created. To use these languages on a Windows-based computer, you will need to install the language and font packs for the languages you need to use.

# D | Extension Manager

With Adobe® Extension Manager, you can create, edit, activate, import, and export plug-ins. After installing the Extension Manager, to access it, select **Help→Manage Extensions**. Extension Manager supports the following:

- User-level extension installation.
- Search and filter extensions.
- MXP to ZXP conversion.
- Extension dependency support.
- Installing extensions when multiple languages of a product are installed.
- Displaying additional extension information.

# Mastery Builders

Mastery Builders are provided for certain lessons as additional learning resources for this course. Mastery Builders are developed for selected lessons within a course in cases when they seem most instructionally useful as well as technically feasible. In general, Mastery Builders are supplemental, optional unguided practice and may or may not be performed as part of the classroom activities. Your instructor will consider setup requirements, classroom timing, and instructional needs to determine which Mastery Builders are appropriate for you to perform, and at what point during the class. If you do not perform the Mastery Builders in class, your instructor can tell you if you can perform them independently as self-study, and if there are any special setup requirements.

# Mastery Builder 1–1
## Preparing a Document for the iPad

**Activity Time: 10 minutes**

### Data File

C:\092024Data\Preparing Documents for Multiple Formats\Playbill Cover Lab.indd

### Scenario

The Scrimdown Playhouse marketing department is developing an iPad application and would like to feature the covers of some of the playbills from the Shakespeare festival.

---

1. Navigate to the folder **C:\092024Data\Preparing Documents for Multiple Formats** and open the file **Playbill Cover Lab.indd**. When prompted to update links, select **Update Modified Links**.

2. Define liquid layout rules for the following objects:
   a) Adjust the Scrimdown Playhouse logo settings so that it does not resize and will remain the same distance from the right edge.
   b) Adjust the green rectangle settings so that it can be resized and keeps the same distance from both the right and left edges, as well as the top edge.
   c) Verify that the Shakespeare image can be resized and remains bleeding off the left and bottom edges.

3. Select **File→Document Setup**. Change the **Intent** to **Mobile**, change the **Page Size** to **iPad**, and change the **Orientation** to **Portrait**.

4. Make manual layout adjustments to the objects. Resize text as necessary.

5. Create an alternate layout for a horizontal orientation.

6. Make manual layout adjustments to the objects. Resize text as necessary.

7. Save the file in the **C:\092024Data\Preparing Documents for Multiple Formats** folder as *My Playbill Cover Lab.indd* and close the file.

---

# Mastery Builder 2-1
## Placing a Graphic in a Document Footer

**Activity Time: 10 minutes**

### Data Files

C:\092024Data\Managing Advanced Page Elements\Sports Brochure Lesson 2 Lab.indd

C:\092024Data\Managing Advanced Page Elements\images\footprints.tif

### Scenario

In an effort to make the brochure for My Footprint Sports more fun and whimsical, you decide to add a footprint icon to the bottom of each page near the page number.

---

1. Navigate to the folder **C:\092024Data\Managing Advanced Page Elements** and open the file **Sports Brochure Lesson 2 Lab.indd**. If prompted to update links, select **Update Modified Links**.

2. Open the **A-Parent** spread.

3. Use the **Rectangle Frame** tool to draw a .3 by .3 square to the right of the text "Keep a running list" on the left page.

4. Place the graphic **C:\092024Data\Managing Advanced Page Elements \images\footprints.tif** in the rectangle using the **Fitting** option **Fit Content to Frame**.

5. Copy the footprint and paste a copy of it to the left side of "Keep a running list" on the right page.

6. Open the spread **2-3** and review the placement of the footprint graphic. Open page **4** and verify the graphic on that page as well.

7. Save the file in the **C:\092024Data\Managing Advanced Page Elements** folder as *My Sports Brochure Lesson 2 Lab.indd* and close it.

---

# Mastery Builder 3-1
## Importing Word Styles into InDesign

**Activity Time: 10 minutes**

### Data Files

C:\092024Data\Managing Styles\Nursery Newsletter Lesson 3 Lab.indd

C:\092024Data\Managing Styles\rewards.docx

### Scenario

In the last newsletter for the school, you included content imported from Microsoft Word. This was very well received, so you've decided to do the same thing again, this time with different content.

---

1. Open **C:\092024Data\Managing Styles\Nursery Newsletter Lesson 3 Lab.indd.** If prompted to update links, select **Update Modified Links**.

2. Using the **Type** tool, import content from **C:\092024Data\Managing Styles\rewards.docx** onto page **5** of the newsletter.

3. In **Microsoft Word Import Options**, map the **Header** and **Normal** styles in the Word document to the **Subheading** and **Body** styles, respectively, in the InDesign document.

4. Verify that imported text in the newsletter has the same style as the original Word doc.

5. Save the file in the **C:\092024Data\Managing Styles** folder as *My Nursery Newsletter Lesson 3 Lab.indd* and close it.

---

# Mastery Builder 4–1
## Creating a Bezier Path

**Activity Time: 10 minutes**

### Data File
C:\092024Data\Building Complex Paths\Nursery Postcard Lesson 4 Lab.indd

### Scenario
You need to create an alternate version of the Greene City Nursery School postcard that emphasizes the upcoming 25th anniversary year. In keeping with the child-centric images, you decide to customize the type for this version.

1. Navigate to the folder **C:\092024Data\Building Complex Paths** and open the file **Nursery Postcard Lesson 4 Lab.indd**. If prompted to update links, select **Update Modified Links**.

2. In the upper left, insert text that reads *Celebrating 25 Years* in **24 pt Times New Roman Regular**.

3. Create type outlines for the "C" in Celebrating.

4. Resize the graphic created by the outline.

5. Apply a gradient to the "C" and apply any other graphic treatments as desired.

6. Save the file in the **C:\092024Data\Building Complex Paths** folder as *My Nursery Postcard Lesson 4 Lab.indd* and close it.

# Mastery Builder 5-1
## Performing a Data Merge

**Activity Time: 10 minutes**

### Data Files

C:\092024Data\Managing External Files and Creating Dynamic Documents\Application Response Letter Lab.indd

C:\092024Data\Managing External Files and Creating Dynamic Documents\applicants.csv

### Scenario

Greene City Nursery School recently posted a job for a new Pre-K teacher. In order to personalize the process, the board decided to send response letters. It is your responsibility to personalize the form letter that will be sent to each of the applicants.

---

1. Navigate to the folder **C:\092024Data\Managing External Files and Creating Dynamic Documents** and open the file **Application Response Letter Lab.indd**.

2. From the **Data Merge** panel options menu, select **Select Data Source** and browse to the file **C:\092024Data\Managing External Files and Creating Dynamic Documents\applicants.csv**.

3. In the line below the text "To:", add placeholders for **Name** and **Street**, each on its own line, then **City** and **State** on a new line, separated by a comma and a space.

4. After the text "Dear", add a placeholder for **Name** and then type a comma.

5. Create the merged document.

6. Review the merged document and then save it in the C:\092024Data\Managing External Files and Creating Dynamic Documents folder as *My Personalized Application Response Letter.indd* and close it.

7. Save and close any other open files.

---

# Mastery Builder 6-1
## Managing Long Documents

**Activity Time: 10 minutes**

### Data Files

C:\092024Data\Managing Long Documents\Lab files\Continents_Africa-v2.indd

C:\092024Data\Managing Long Documents\Lab files\Continents_Antarctica-v2.indd

C:\092024Data\Managing Long Documents\Lab files\Continents_Australia-v2.indd

C:\092024Data\Managing Long Documents\Lab files\Continents_Eurasia-v2.indd

C:\092024Data\Managing Long Documents\Lab files\Continents_NorthAmerica-v2.indd

C:\092024Data\Managing Long Documents\Lab files\Continents_SouthAmerica-v2.indd

### Scenario

The content of the travel book you created last year has been updated, and the publisher would like you to again combine all the individual documents into a single file.

1. In InDesign, create a new book file named *My Travel Book.indb* and save it to the C:\92024Data\Managing Long Documents\Lab files folder.

2. From C:\92024Data\Managing Long Documents\Lab files, add the v2 documents for the six continents to the book.

3. In the **My Travel Book** panel, verify that the content for all the continents appears.

4. In the **Continents_Africa-v2** file, on page 1, using the **Layout** menu, create a table of contents with a style of your choosing. If a table of contents already exists, change its formatting to a different style.

5. Verify that the table of contents appears with the proper styles and page numbers.

6. Save the file in the C:\92024Data\Managing Long Documents\Lab files folder as *My Travel Book.indd* and close it.

# Mastery Builder 7-1
## Exporting PDF Files for Print

**Activity Time: 10 minutes**

### Data File
C:\092024Data\Publishing InDesign Files for Other Formats and Customizing Print Settings\Flyer.indd

### Scenario
The manager at Scrimdown Playhouse really loves the flyer you created. He has asked you to export it into different formats for distribution.

---

1. Open the file **C:\092024Data\Publishing InDesign Files for Other Formats and Customizing Print Settings\Flyer.indd**.

2. Export the flyer as an **Adobe PDF (Print)**. In the **Output** section, convert the color to grayscale.

3. View the PDF and verify that it is grayscale.

4. Now export the file as a color PDF with printer marks including crop marks, registration marks, page information, and all bleed settings set to **.25**.

5. View the PDF to verify that the output is as expected.

6. Export the file as **HTML**, with the **Image Alignment** set to **Align Left**.

7. Examine the exported file using a browser.

8. Close all open files. Discard any changes to **Flyer.indd**.

9. Close InDesign.

---

# Solutions

5. **Why do some pages have the new numbering and some don't?**

   A: Pages **2** and **4** have the parent **B-Left** applied, which is based on **A-Parent**. Pages **3** and **5** are based on **B-Right** parent which is not based on **A-Parent**.

# Glossary

**absolute page numbering**
A type of page numbering where the pages are numbered sequentially.

**anchored object**
Any object that has a link to a text frame.

**Bezier path**
A path that contains one or more anchor points with direction handles to adjust the size of the path.

**book**
A file that comprises more than one document.

**clipping path**
A path that is used to hide the outside areas of an image and make the inside area visible.

**color management**
The process of controlling software and hardware to match colors between devices such as a computer monitor and a printer.

**color separation**
The process of breaking up the different colors in an artwork onto different printing plates.

**compound path**
A path that contains more than one path and intersects to form a hole.

**data merge**
An InDesign feature that can be used to create data by merging data from two different files.

**document pages**
InDesign pages that are created for laying out text and graphical objects.

**embedded clipping path**
A clipping path that is imported from other applications.

**flattening**
A process that divides transparent objects into vector-based and raster-based areas in an artwork.

**footnote**
A note that is associated with text on a page and is placed at the bottom of the page.

**hyperlink**
A link that enables users to move to another location.

**hyphenation**
A process of inserting hyphens in between the syllables of a word so that when the text is justified, maximum space is utilized.

**index**
A list of words in a document and their associated page numbers.

**inline graphic**
A graphic that appears along with the text, usually with the description.

**interactive document**
A document that allows you to navigate to linked pages.

**justification**
A paragraph option to control the spacing between letters of a word.

**keep options**
A feature that allows you to keep lines of a paragraph together and specify break links in a line.

**kern pairs**
A pair of letters with spacing already adjusted.

**kerning**
A character format used to adjust the space between specific letter pairs.

**layer comps**
Different forms of an image that are stored in a file.

**library**
A storage location which is mainly used for reusing components.

**metrics kerning**
A character format used to adjust the space between kern pairs.

**nested style**
A style that allows you to apply character-level formatting to specific ranges of text within a paragraph.

**optical kerning**
A character format used to adjust the space between characters of different font or size.

**overprint**
A technique that displays the top-most color of overlapping shapes as transparent, thereby displaying the corner edges of the areas underneath.

**overprint preview**
A command that is used to identify problems during printing.

**pagination**
The consecutive numbering or organization of content in a document according to the specified settings.

**parent page**
A virtual page that appears by default whenever a new document is created and where you can store objects or items which can be applied to all the pages in a document.

**Presentation mode**
A view that displays an active document as a presentation.

**print presets**
Print job settings saved to determine the print output of a file.

**process color**
A color that is a combination of any or all of the standard colors: cyan, magenta, yellow, and black.

**scaling**
A character format used to specify the height and width of text.

**section**
A portion of the document that is meant for holding document items such as an index or a preface.

**section page numbering**
A type of page numbering where you specify the page number preceded by a section name.

**spot color**
A color that allows you to print objects with a single ink.

**style override**
The format applied to text that is already formatted using a style.

**style redefining**
A feature that allows you to change the attributes of an existing style.

**table of contents**
An item that helps users find information quickly.

**tracking**
Adjusting the space between the letters within a selection.

## transparency

An effect created by adjusting the opacity of an object.

## trapping

The process of expanding objects to fill gaps between different colors of overlapping objects.

## type outline

An outline created from an existing path where you can adjust the shape of the type to a wide range of sizes.

## widows and orphans

Words or single lines of text that are separated from the rest of the paragraph.

## XHTML

(eXtensible Hypertext Markup Language) An HTML markup language that is defined as an XML application.

# Index